Baby Heart

Emily Allen Garland

authorHOUSE®

AuthorHouse™
1663 Liberty Drive, Suite 200
Bloomington, IN 47403
www.authorhouse.com
Phone: 1-800-839-8640

First published by AuthorHouse 2/27/2009

ISBN: 978-1-4389-4835-5 (sc)

Printed in the United States of America
Bloomington, Indiana

This book is printed on acid-free paper.

Other books by this author:
Giving a Voice to the Ancestors
Bittersweet Memories- A Memoir

Honey, you planted the seed that grew into Baby Heart. Thanks for your inspiration.

Acknowledgements

Thanks to all of my West Bloomfield Writer's Group members, with a special thanks to our leader, Fran Knorr. You showed your love for Baby Heart and by doing so made bringing her to life for me easy and enjoyable.

The members of my PASAWAR Writers Group were equally as enthusiastic about Baby Heart. Thanks for your help and support. Dan Callahan's insightful and knowledgeable guidance was extremely helpful to the development of this, my first novel.

Wynter Cuthbert, author of Eliza's Dream: A Memoir of a Southern Soul has been generous with her support. Thanks, Wynter.

Prologue

I wake up every morning at four o'clock in a cold sweat. The same nightmare has plagued me for more years than I have left to live. I feel the bullet pierce my heart. I clutch my chest; feel blood ooze between my fingers. It has a metallic smell.

My other hand has a death grip on the steering wheel. I feel no pain, yet I know I must die. A bullet just entered my heart. No way can I survive. Then I see the gleam of the gray steel pistol pointed at my ten-year-old son. He screams at the same time I hear the blast.

> We can't die here like this. My girls — both of them —are in the backseat with my son. I turn the key in the ignition, the motor turns over — **vroom**. I hold tight to the steering wheel, and push down on the gas pedal with all my strength. I'm a dying woman zooming along a Georgia highway at breakneck speed until a patrolman pulls me over.

The shade of darkness begins its descent slowly, quietly, covering me in black velvety softness.

1

AUGUST 1946

I love Papa Joe. I go with him to the field to plant potato slips in the spring, chop cotton in July and pick it at the end of summer. Today my bag is heavy with cotton when I call out to him. He's a row over and quite a bit closer to the end of his row than I am to mine, "Papa Joe, I been thinking. I sure wanna go to school in town."

He straightens up, wipes his eyes and brow with the colorful kerchief he uses as a sweat rag. His long black braids hang from under his straw hat. He looks directly at me. "I know you do, Baby Heart. But you done finished seventh grade. Most other girls ain't got nearly that far."

"Papa Joe, that's just the girls out here in White Chalk. Girls finish high school in Marysville every June and go on to be teachers, nurses

1

and such. That's what I want to be —a nurse and take care of sick folks." Two heavy, long black braids hang over each shoulder and down to my waist. I straighten up and mop my brow with the back of my hand. Sweat pours down my reddish brown face. The dress I have on — made from the flowered bags that chicken feed comes in —clings to my fourteen year old well-developed body. The sun blazes down on us without mercy and the heat shimmers in the air like floating silvery wings.

"I know, Baby Heart. But we just country folks. You hafta have money to room and board in town. We don't have no kinfolk over there you can stay with."

"My friend Candy told me she knows some folk in town. She's gonna stay with her mama's second cousin. The lady's name is Trudy Miller. She thinks Miz Miller might have room for me."

"Sho nuff? Well, how we gonna pay her?"

I know I have Papa Joe's attention now. I lug my nearly full crocus bag of cotton, draped across my shoulders, up even to him. "Papa Joe, Candy says her cousin likely will accept food instead of money. If you carry sweet potatoes, a chicken or some ham and such every Sunday when I go to stay the week …"

Joe Turner, that's my papa's full name, looks at me with a frown. "You done skipped some cotton. Go on back down that row to where you left off. Give me time to think about this. I don't know why you so hepped up on goin' to school. You oughta be thinkin' 'bout gettin married like yo' sistahs done."

"Papa Joe, I been thinking about them and marriage. That's why I wanna go to school so bad. Irene got married when she was fifteen. Look at her now, a house full of children, a drunken husband beating on her half the time. Is that what you want for me?" My voice chokes and the words come out all croaky. I'm almost in tears.

"Baby Heart, you know out of all eight of my chirren, you my heart. I wants better for my baby girl, and I knows how to get it. John El Murphy got his eyes on you. He been noticing you for a long time, just waitin' for you to grow up so he can approach you proper. He tole me how he feels about you, and asked my permission to come courtin' soon as you turn fifteen."

I take the sack from my back and throw it to the ground. "Papa Joe, you serious? You think I want John El? He's old enough to be my daddy."

"He's older for sho. But he can take care of you in style. John El Murphy is the richest colored man in these parts. He owns the chalk mine, general store and most of the houses in White Chalk."

I place my hands on my hips and stand flatfooted looking him straight in the eye. Tears form and cling to my eyelids. I refuse to let them fall. I have to be strong like a man to make him hear me. I can't be a crybaby or whine like Mama Lilly and get my way with Papa Joe. I know that much about him. "Papa Joe, I don't want no man taking care of me. I want a education so I can be independent and take care of myself."

He clears his throat and turns his head away from me. "Well, I never said I wouldn't look into the school thing. But don't get yo' hopes too high. I doubt if anybody is gonna take you in for nine months for the few rations we can spare."

"Papa Joe, just promise you'll speak to Candy's cousin. And don't encourage Mr. Murphy. I've seen the way he's been looking at me lately. I don't want nothing to do with him."

Before we weigh our cotton, we make sure there ain't no hulls clinging to it. Mr. Murphy subtracts a big penalty amount if he finds hulls and stems. They add falsely to the weight, he claims. 'It's the same as stealing,' I heard him tell Papa Joe.

John El Murphy owns the land we farm as well as the rundown three- room shack we live in. Papa Joe is right. John El owns most everything and everybody in White Chalk. He don't cut nobody no slack because he's colored same as the rest of us. John El always says 'it's all about bitniz.'

Once people get in John El's debt, they never get out. Only a few have been brave enough to run off owing him. His wife ran off many years ago and John El never married again. Some folks whisper that she might not have run away at all. John El may have killed her and planted her body on some of the hundreds of acres surrounding his house. He's so mean; I believe he coulda killed her. But worse of all, I hear some folks whisper that he's waiting for me to grow up so he can marry me.

Papa Joe and I head to John El's general store where he's got a cotton gin out back.

The wagon wheels clonk along on the dry, rutty red clay road that like everything else in White Chalk is covered with a film of white dust from the chalk mine.

When he sees us coming, he jumps up from a bench on the unpainted porch - gray from age and the weather - and walks over to meet the wagon. He squints his eyes real tight. I can hardly see the pale green of his eyeballs. John El is a runt, only about five-five. The big gun that he wears in plain view on his hip makes him appear much taller to most folks. His skin is yellow. I notice the creases around his neck. He looks like a cracker to me — a mean one at that. Mama Lilly say his daddy was a white man who left all his property, including the chalk mine, to John El when he died some years back.

"Howdy, Big Joe. Got some cotton for me today?" John El asks.

"Sho nuff. I got over a bale here. Me and Baby Heart made sho ain't no hulls in it."

I burrow down, trying to hide under the soft, fluffy white cotton. John El walks around to the side of the wagon and pushes the cotton off my face. "Who you hiding from, Baby Heart? Get on outta that wagon unless you wanta get ginned with the cotton."

I crawl out from underneath the cotton, jump down from the wagon and brush the lint off my dress. His eyes open wide and I can feel them all over me.

He walks around to Papa Joe who is sitting in the driver's seat holding onto the reins to keep the mule still. "When's her fifteenth birthday, Joe?"

Papa Joe looks around at me with a sad expression, hangs his head and says, "October twenty-third,"

"Bring the cotton on 'round back, Joe. Baby Heart, you go inside the store and get yo'self a cold bottle of soda water. That's my treat for you." He smiles and walks around behind the store to the cotton gin.

I'm hot and thirsty but I don't want no treats from John El Murphy. No Sir Ree. I sit down on the bench out front and wait. I know Papa Joe will collect little, if any money from the cotton after John El subtracts his outstanding debt. The dollar or two that he gets goes right back to the general store for tobacco, rations and a little corn liquor sold on the sly by John El.

On the way home, I sit on the seat next to Papa Joe. "Why did you tell him when my birthday comes?"

"I tole you already. He wants to come callin' when you turn fifteen."

"Papa Joe, I'll kill myself before I let that mean old man touch me!"

I say it with such force till I suppose he believes me because he clears his throat and says, "Baby Heart, ask Candy to 'range for me

5

to meet with her cousin. If she'll take you in, you can start school in Marysville next month. It ain't fair for you to hafta pay our debts."

I grab Papa Joe and hug him real tight. When we get home Mama Lilly is sitting on the front porch in our old rocking chair— the one with cardboard replacing the worn-out straw bottom. She gets up slowly, smiling, glad to see us.

We all go inside together. She has supper ready; biscuits, fried pork shoulder and pear preserves. Coffee is brewing on the wood- burning stove. Nothing smells better to me than strong coffee when it's brewing. I pour myself a cup. The tantalizing aroma is way better than the taste. I get up from the bench where I was sitting at our rough wooden kitchen table and give the coffee to Papa Joe. I know he can drink two cups. I pour a glass of buttermilk and sit back down, eager to share my news with Mama Lilly.

She's pale and thin. Her hair, mostly gray, is pulled into a little knot on top of her head. She looks old and worn out. Eight children and four miscarriages did that to her, I think. I compare her now to pictures around the house when she was young and pretty. I promise myself right then, no man is gonna fill me with babies, causing me to lose my looks and grow old before my time.

"Guess what, Mama Lilly?"

"What? She asks listlessly.

"Papa Joe told me I can go to school in town next month. I'm sure I have a place to stay. I'm going to finish high school and go to college to be a nurse, Mama Lilly!"

She looks at me and bursts out crying.

"What's the matter, Mama Lilly? Don't you want me to go?"

"These happy tears, Baby Heart. At last one of my chirren gonna make something out of herself." Mama Lilly pulls me into her arms. I snuggle close to her for a while, taking in the sweet scent of her talcum powder mixed with the smell of coffee and pork shoulder.

SEPTEMBER 1946

I walk into the Eighth Grade classroom in Marysville with one long, black heavy braid hanging down to my butt. It's the same thing everywhere I go if folks haven't seen me before. Boys and some men too, look at me with eyes popping out of their sockets, while girls turn green with envy. I know the boys are staring at my body as I look for a empty seat. I wish my breasts would slow down growing. I try not to switch when I walk but my hips, that seem to get rounder every day, sway anyhow.

Self-consciously, I find my way to a seat. I'm glad Candy is right behind me. We sit down beside each other and try not to look around at the other students who continue to stare— mostly at me.

Marysville High for Colored isn't all I'd thought it would be but it is better than the one- room church school I went to since I was six years old. Grades one through seven were all in the same room with two teachers for all those different grades and ages. Somehow I learned. I admired my teachers and I try to talk like them and how they taught me. It isn't easy. Some folks say I sound too proper, that I'm putting on airs. So I keep saying ain't and ya'll even though I know it's wrong.

Soon, I will find out if I learned enough to keep up in a real school with desks and blackboards. There are different rooms and teachers for different classes at Marysville High. We change classrooms when the bell rings. There is no auditorium and science lab like I read about white schools having — no gym or indoor toilets even, but it is way ahead of the church school.

The bell rings for recess at noon. Candy and I go outside with our brown paper lunch bags filled with peanut butter and jelly sandwiches and apples. We find a grassy hill under a shade tree and sit down. About six girls walk over and stand in front of us. The leader puts her hands on her hips and proceeds to dog us out.

"Y'all stuck up or something? Think you too good to mix with us 'cause you got that straight, long hair hanging down yo' back?" she asks, looking right at me.

"We glad to talk with y'all. We ain't stuck up," I say. Even though it's clear they want to make trouble instead of friends.

A girl with short, greasy messy looking hair asks me, "Where you get all that long hair from? It looks like a horses tail. Did you cut a mules tail and pin it on yo' head?"

I toss my head proudly and don't back down one bit. "I got it from my daddy. He wears his hair in long braids like this too, same as his daddy who's a Indian."

"Oh, so you a Indian?" The girl asks me with nasty attitude

dripping from each word.

"I didn't say I'm no Indian. You asked where my hair come from and I just told you."

Candy breaks in, "Jolee is my best friend. She's a real nice girl. Why don't y'all get to know us before you decide we stuck up?"

They're ready to turn on Candy, who's a lighter complexion than I am, with short curly hair, when we see a bunch of boys heading our way. As they come closer, I notice that the one leading the pack is cute. Sho nuff good-looking. He has a straight keen nose, big muscles in his chest and arms. His black hair is soft and curly; his skin, like deep rich chocolate. He walks right over to me and says, "My name's Bobby Miller. I saw you come in this morning. Can I walk you back to class?"

"Yeah, I, I guess so," I stutter. "My name's Jolee Turner but my folks and close friends call me by my nickname, Baby Heart."

The other girls, except Candy, look at me with daggers shooting out of their eyes. One of them says real loud, "Bobby Joe is Mattie Mae's boyfriend. Wait 'til she finds out. She'll whip yo' ass."

Bobby Joe takes my hand in his as we walk toward the school. "Don't listen to them. I don't have a girlfriend. I'm hoping we can get to know each other. Maybe you will be my girl, Baby Heart." He looks down and smiles at me. His teeth are even and pearly white.

I feel myself drifting with the current, being swept away on my first day of school in Marysville. I've never seen a boy I liked before. Never had a boyfriend. Yet, this boy just walks up to me, announces that he wants me to be his girl and I feel something I never felt before — something exciting. The whole world suddenly seems new. Everything around me is different. The sky is bluer than it ever looked before, the grass greener. I never knew how sweet the magnolia and jasmine blossoms smelled before today. Birds dip and sway as they fly overhead. I listen and hear them singing just for Bobby and me.

When the bell rings at the end of the school day, I'm not surprised when I see him waiting for me outside the door. He takes my books and asks if he can walk me home. I look around for Candy but another boy is walking besides her, carrying her books.

"Where do you live?" Bobby asks.

"I'm boarding with Miz Miller, Candy's cousin. I live in White Chalk."

"Miz Trudy Miller?"

"Uh huh. Y'all got the same last name. Are you kin to her?"

"Sorta. She's my aunt-in-law. My uncle, who was married to her, is dead. She's still my favorite Auntie."

Bobby walks in the house with me like he owns it calling out, "Aunt Trudy!"

Miz Miller is all smiles. She hugs him and says, "Sit down and have some sweet potato pie and milk with us."

"Thanks, but I'm really not hungry, Auntie."

"I see you met Jolee. Where's Candy, Jolee?"

"She's right behind us, Miz Miller," I say.

She looks at Bobby and me. I think she sees the sparks flying between us. She chuckles and tells Bobby "It's a good thing you're taking a fancy to Jolee instead of Candy, 'cause Candy's your cousin."

"Not really. She's your cousin."

"Well, what's mine is yours" she says and throws her head back with a hearty laugh.

I like Miz Miller right off. She's a happy-go-lucky plump lady who's full of life. She treats us like a mother but has a whole lot more energy than Mama Lilly. She owns the only beauty shop for colored ladies in Marysville. Three other beauticians work in her shop. They stay busy keeping the ladies of the town pretty.

Miz Miller tells Candy and me that she needs two shampoo girls. The girls she had working for her graduated in June and left for college this month. Both Candy and I jump for joy at the opportunity to work. I can pay for my room and board without Papa Joe having to worry about bringing rations. Even better, I'm relieved of the other worry that keeps gnawing at my mind. If I stay in town on the weekends, John El Murphy can't come courting when I turn fifteen next month.

Candy and I ride the bus back to White Chalk at the end of my first week in high school. We're both eager to break the news to our parents about Miz Miller's offer of work.

"Papa Joe, Mama Lilly— guess what?" I ask while we're sitting around the kitchen table after dinner.

"I can't guess what but it must be somethin' good judgin' by that big grin on yo' face," Papa Joe says.

"Miz Miller wants Candy and me to work in her beauty shop, shampooing hair on Friday evenings and all day Saturdays. We can make enough money to take care of our room and board and have some money left over for clothes and allowance."

A sad expression crosses their faces for a minute and then it lifts like sunshine bursting through a cloud. "We happy for you, Baby Heart," Mama Lilly says.

"I didn't want to tell you, but it was goin' to put a strain on me tryin' to bring rations to town on Sundays. We gonna miss you, though." Papa Joe sighs and looks away.

"You and Mama Lilly can stop by the beauty parlor on Saturdays when you come into town."

"We don't want to shame you, ridin' up in front of a fancy beauty parlor in a wagon, yo' daddy in overalls and me in a plain old cotton housedress."

"Mama Lilly, Papa Joe —I don't want to hear y'all say nothin' like that ever again. I love y'all more than anything and I'm proud of y'all. I'll be happy to show my parents to the whole town. I don't care what people think."

Papa Joe pulls out his Bull Durham tobacco, takes a paper leaf from his pack, and commences to roll a cigarette, all the while studying my face like he wants to say something but is wondering if he should. After a good bit of silence in the room, he says to me "John El Murphy asked about you, offered to drive y'all back to town Sunday evening. He said I could go along to chaperone."

"Papa Joe, I'll ride to town beside you in the wagon with my head held high. But I refuse to ride anywhere with John El Murphy. I told you before and I'll tell you again, I don't want nothing to do with Mr. John El Murphy. Not Now. Not Ever. We'll catch the bus back to town." I walk out on the front porch and slam the screen door behind me. The very mention of his name spoils all of my happiness. I sit on the step and think about Bobby Joe until I begin to feel good again.

I'm happy to be home with Papa Joe and Mama Lilly. She cooks a big country breakfast Sunday morning; fried chicken smothered in onion gravy, country ham, grits, biscuits and preserves. My sister, Irene and her brood of kids come over for breakfast. Looks like it's the first good meal they had in a long time. Irene is frail with a bruise under her right eye and the kids are scrawny. A baby is nursing at her breast.

The eight-month-old baby is cute as a button. I'm very fond of her and start everybody calling her Cherub because she reminds me of the pictures of the little baby angels I see on the paper fans in church. She's plump and dimpled with brown hair in big ringlets.

When I ask Irene where Willie Lee is, she shakes her head and a tear rolls down her cheek. I'm sorry I asked about her old mean husband. The sight of Irene causes a shadow to darken the daydreams I was having of Bobby Joe and me. If this is what marriage brings about, I don't want no part of it — not even with Bobby Joe.

I'm having the best time of my life in Marysville. I catch right on to the classes with the help of Bobby Joe. He's in the tenth grade, smart as a whiz and captain of the football team. He's the star of Marysville High. After the other students see that I'm his girl, they all want to be my friends.

I'm popular, in love with a boy who loves me and I'm making money at the beauty shop. In addition to our pay from Miz Miller, most of the customers tip us for washing their hair.

I write to Papa Joe and Mama Lilly and get permission to stay on in Marysville for Thanksgiving. School is closed Friday. So Candy and I get to work two full days. Miz Miller is already hoping we can stay with her in the summer and work full time. I have it all planned. I will save most of the extra money for college. But I feel like I need to go home for the Christmas Holidays. I'm beginning to miss my folks. And I feel a little guilty because I'm having such a good time when I know they're hurting, especially Irene and her kids.

CHRISTMAS 1946

Papa Joe and I do the same thing every Christmas Eve. We always walk into the woods to find a Christmas tree. I get to pick it. He chops it down and drags it home. We sing Christmas carols all the time we're looking for the perfect tree. I usually choose a pine tree because I like that clean crisp scent of pine in the house on Christmas morning. But a pretty round, plump cedar catches my eye and I tell Papa Joe, "This is the one right here. It's shaped perfect."

"You sho, Baby Heart? You ain't gonna miss the pine scent?" White smoke floats from his mouth when his breath meets the cold frosty air.

I like the cold weather and wish it would snow. I know it won't though. It hardly ever snows in Georgia. I only saw a trace of the white stuff once in my life.

"I'm sure Papa Joe." I say holding on to his hand.

We drag the tree home, laughing and singing all the way, "Oh, what fun it is to ride in a one horse open sleigh." I can only imagine what that would feel like. But it sounds like fun and Papa Joe and I like to sing that carol.

When we get home, Mama Lilly is in the kitchen making a cake. Papa Joe puts the tree up in the front room while I get the decorations from under the bed. We use the same ones every year —a few ornaments passed down by a white lady Mama Lilly used to work for and a pretty angel for the top of the tree my grandmother gave us many years ago. Papa Joe always adds peppermint sticks for the children.

I'm still decorating the tree and humming Christmas Carols when I hear Mama Lilly start coughing a dry hacking cough that seems not to want to end. I go in the kitchen where I find her slumped over the table still coughing. "Mama Lilly, what's the matter? Do you have any cough medicine?"

She points toward her bedroom. I run in and look on her dresser and come right back with the cough syrup. I pour a spoon-full and get it in her mouth between coughs.

"Mama Lilly, you go rest. I'll finish the cake. It's that darned old white dust from John El's chalk mine that's got you and half of the folks around here coughing yourselves to death."

She speaks in a raspy voice after she takes the cough medicine. "I better stay here and make sure you mix that cake right."

"I can do it, Mama Lilly. I wrote everything down last time I watched you make cakes. Go on and get some rest before you start coughing again."

She looks so sad and worn as she turns and starts into her room with a lit kerosene lamp in her hand. I run over and take it from her and go ahead of her. I'm afraid she may have another coughing fit and drop it, causing a fire. I really am worried about Mama Lilly. I see for the first time that she's failing.

Christmas day starts out happy.

I get up early like I always do on Christmas morning. Papa Joe and Mama Lilly are still in bed. The house is cold because he hasn't lit a fire yet. I like it this way. I can see my breath on the air and take in the smell of the cedar tree that's stronger because the house is cold. The scent of oranges and apples mixed with cedar fill the air. Christmas morning is the only time fresh fruit is in our house in winter. Mama Lilly cans fruit in the summer so we can eat preserves and make pies in the cold weather. We will give the fresh fruit to Irene's children when they come over. It's unlikely that they have any treats at their house.

I start a fire in the kitchen stove. I'm rolling dough for the biscuits when Papa Joe comes in the kitchen.

"Merry Christmas, Baby Heart." He hugs me and says, "I didn't have much money for presents, but here's a little somethin' for my baby girl."

He hands me a small package wrapped in Christmas gift paper. I unwrap it and place the red comb in my hair. I give Papa Joe a big kiss on the cheek. "I got something for you, too. I'll give it to you after breakfast." I think about how happy he will be when he sees the new shirt I bought him. I have some toilet water and a gown for Mama Lilly.

Mama Lilly looks a little better when she comes out bundled

in a pink flannel robe one of my brothers gave her last Christmas. Before we get finished with our breakfast of ham, eggs, grits and biscuits, she starts coughing again and gets up from the table. Papa Joe looks worried as he watches her leave the room. "How long has she been like this?" I ask him.

"The hard coughin' started in aroun' Thanksgiving. I thought it was just a chest cold. But it don't seem to be lettin' up none."

"Maybe you should take her to the doctor."

"I'll see about it after Christmas."

After I wash the breakfast dishes and give Mama Lilly and Papa Joe their gifts, I head over to my sister Irene's. I love all of my nieces and nephews but I'm dying to see her baby, my little Cherub.

The little ones see me coming. They run up the path to meet me. Little Cherub—who wasn't walking last time I saw her— toddles behind her brothers and sister. I run to meet them and scoop her up in one arm. My other hand holds tight to the bag of gifts for them.

Irene is standing in the kitchen with one eye swollen nearly shut. I hug her close. "Merry Christmas, Irene."

"Merry Christmas, Baby Heart." She doesn't sound merry at all. The dress she's wearing is old and torn.

The children tug at the bag in my hand. I open it and hand each one a gift wrapped in brightly colored paper. Their faces light up like the sun coming out after a long rainy day. James, the four-year-old, unwraps a small shiny tinhorn and starts tooting it. Charley Boy, eight, puts the new harmonica to his mouth and begins to play. Camilla looks through her coloring book and crayons. Cherub giggles and clutches the toy lamb on wheels. I show her how to pull it behind her. It plays "Mary Had a Little Lamb." She pulls it over the rough wooden floor, laughing and stopping every now and then to clap her little hands gleefully.

James runs over and grabs it from her. A ruckus breaks out. Cherub shrieks a piercing high- pitched cry. "James, give her toy back," I holler.

He runs around the room pulling it and laughing loudly. The other two join in the fun.

The door to the only bedroom in the house opens and Willie Lee, all bleary-eyed bursts into the kitchen. "Why in the hell can't you keep these younguns quiet, Irene? You know I'm tryin' to sleep."

His foul breath fogs up the room. The stale sweetish odor of white lighting oozes from his pores.

Irene smiles, "Oh, Willie Lee, it's Christmas mornin.' Can't the kids have a little fun?"

"Not when I'm tryin' to sleep. Quiet 'em down or else all of y'all can get out."

"You got some nerve, Willie Lee. You stayed down to that still drinkin' and gamblin' all night. Now you want yo' chirren quiet as mice on Christmas mornin.' You oughta be glad somebody gave them some presents. You ain't paid Santa to bring them a dadgum thing." Irene turns her back to him.

The children crouch quietly in a corner with big frightened eyes fixed on their daddy.

Willie Lee looks at me with his old red eyes, "Baby Heart can get her ass on out of here. She think she somethin' on a stick 'cause she goin' to school in town."

Irene says to the children, "Y'all can play if you want too."

Willie Lee darts across the room faster than I can catch my breath.

"Who you think you is, woman? Contradictin' me in my own house." His fist slams into the one eye Irene can see out of. The other one is swollen almost shut from their last fight.

She picks up a piece of stove wood and strikes back, as frail and battered as she is. The children begin howling. I pick Cherub up along with her lamb and tell the other kids, "ya'll come on home with me. Papa Joe got some fruit and candy canes up at the house."

Charley Boy runs along beside me as we hurry through the woods. "I wish I was older. I would kill him. He's always beatin' on Mama," he says.

"Now, Charley Boy it's Christmas morning and Willie Lee is your daddy. Don't talk like that."

"Soon as I can shoulder a rifle I'm gonna kill him, Baby Heart."

The sacred feeling of Christmas morning is shattered. We run in the door out of breath. The younger children holler at the top of their lungs while snot runs from their noses.

Papa Joe is standing in the kitchen when we run in. "What's the matter?" He asks.

"Willie Lee is still half drunk from last night. He jumped on Irene and punched her in the eye again."

Papa Joe is a big man, over six feet tall, and weighs about two hundred pounds with broad shoulders. He grabs the rifle that he uses to kill a rabbit for dinner now and again and heads out the door. I hear him say, "I'm tired of that sorry no good bastard beatin' on my daughter."

I put the children out on the front porch with a shoebox full of apples, oranges and nuts. The sun is shining and it's warm enough for them to play outside in the thin jackets they're wearing. "Charley Boy, watch over your sisters and brother. Don't let them wander off." I tell him.

"I will, Baby Heart. You think Papa Joe is gonna kill my daddy?" Charley Boy has a frightened look in his eyes.

"No, Charley Boy. Papa Joe hates to kill a rabbit. He may scare some sense into him, though."

I heat up some water and take it in my room to wash up. I get clean and put on the pretty red skirt and green sweater my brother, Roosevelt sent me for Christmas from Boston where he lives now with his wife and children. I look in the cloudy dresser mirror while I comb my hair. I leave it loose and tuck the red comb Papa Joe gave me for Christmas in to hold my long wavy hair to one side. I approve of the image smiling at me in the mirror. I put on some lipstick and I'm ready. Papa Joe and Irene come in the backdoor and I hear them go into the other bedroom where Mama Lilly is resting. Irene is sobbing and saying, "I ain't ever goin' back to him agin."

I walk over to the other room. She looks awful. I hug her. "You okay, Irene?"

"I'll be fine, Baby Heart."

Papa Joe looks me over. "Where you goin,' Baby Heart?"

"I thought I'd go over to Candy's for a while, if it's all right with you and Mama Lilly."

"You sho nuff look pretty. Go on, but be back here 'fore dark. I don't want you walkin' through these woods in the nighttime."

"Yes sir."

I light out up the road, glad to be getting away from all of the confusion going on at my house. I love Irene and the children but I need some merriment on Christmas day.

As I round the bend to Candy's house, I see a car parked in her yard. My heart begins to beat ninety miles an hour. I wonder if Bobby Joe really came. He asked if he could come to see me Christmas day. He wasn't sure if he could find a way. No busses run between Marysville and White Chalk on holidays. So, I doubted he would make it. I told him in case he did find a way, to come to Candy's house. I had a feeling my house would be busy with my sisters and brothers and kids all over the place.

Candy comes to the door as soon as I knock. She hugs me and says, "I have a surprise for you."

Bobby Joe is standing behind the door. We hug and kiss for the longest. I forget about everything else — about Mama Lilly's cough, about Irene and the possibility John El Murphy may come calling tonight; another reason I wanted to get away from my house.

4

CHRISTMAS EVENING 1946

"Bobby Joe, where'd you get a car?"

"I borrowed my brother's. I can't stay too long. He's gonna need it later on this evening. Wanna go for a ride?"

Candy's mama hears us talking and comes bustling into the front room. "Not before y'all eat. I wouldn't dare have my cousin Trudy's favorite nephew come all the way out here on Christmas day and not feed him. Specially since she's taking such good care of Candy and Baby Heart."

We sit down to dinner of roast chicken and dressing, collard greens, candied sweet potatoes, and home made rolls. Then she brings out what we all love most: sweet potato pie, coconut cake, chocolate cake and sweet milk. Bobby Joe and I sit side by side, smiling at each other while we eat— happy in love on Christmas day. After dinner we leave and ride to a deserted road so we can have some time to ourselves.

Bobby Joe pulls out a pretty gift-wrapped box and hands it to me. "Merry Christmas, Baby Heart."

I open the box and see the prettiest thing I think I've ever seen, a gold compact with a diamond teardrop on the front. I know it's only gold plated and the diamond is really rhinestone, but it's beautiful. Bobby Joe's love and tenderness shines through causing a real teardrop of joy and happiness to roll down my cheek.

He pulls me in his arms. "Why are you crying, Baby Heart?"

"It's so beautiful. It's pure like our love."

"I wish I could give you more. One day I will give you real diamonds."

I straighten up. "Bobby Joe, I left your gift in town. I wasn't sure you were coming. I can't give it to you until I come back to Marysville."

"Baby Heart, don't you know the only gift I want is you? Can I have you?"

"You already have me— for now, for always." I plant a kiss on his lips.

He's breathing hard as he whispers in my ear, "I want to show you how much I love you."

"I know what you want, Bobby Joe. I can't give it to you now."

"Why not?"

"Good girls don't do that until they marry."

"Nobody will know but us."

"Yeah, until I get pregnant and have to go marching up in front of the church begging forgiveness."

"Baby Heart, do you really think I would put you through something like that? I love you. I have a rubber. I'll protect you and if something happens, I'll marry you."

"Bobby Joe, I'm not ready for that. If you really love me you'll wait."

He squeezes my hand and looks into my eyes. "Baby Heart, I'll wait for you forever if I have to. I better get you home now."

"Yeah, first dusk is falling. I promised Papa Joe I would be home before dark."

"Do I get to meet your folks?"

"Sure. It may take an hour for you to meet them all. I have four sisters and two brothers who still live in White Chalk. They will probably all be there with about twenty kids between them."

I hear a car behind us as we drive home. I'm not sure where it's going until we turn onto the road leading directly to my house. The car turns too. I look back and there he is— John El Murphy driving his new green Cadillac. He's not in the habit of visiting my family on Christmas day. I know what this means.

I want to tell Bobby Joe to turn around and take me back to Candy's, but there's no room to turn. He keeps his car squarely behind Bobby Joe's. I want to tell Bobby all about John El and how scared I am but my tongue feels like it's stuck to the roof of my mouth. I just sit there until we get to my house.

Bobby Joe gets out and begins to walk around to open my door. John El beats him to it. He yanks the door open and yells, "Who's this nigger you ridin' aroun' with?"

I jump out of the car; place my hands on my hips. My blood is boiling. Unafraid, I find my tongue. "He ain't no nigger. He's my boyfriend. What business of yours is it who I ride around with?"

"I told your daddy I was comin' to see you this evening. He's on my time now. So that makes it my bitniz."

"You didn't ask me if you could come."

Bobby Joe is standing here with his mouth open. Now he says, "Mister, I don't know who you are, but this is my girl and I don't like what you just said."

John El pulls his jacket back far enough to show the pearl handle of his revolver. He squints at Bobby Joe and puts one hand on the gun. "Boy, you better get in your car, turn it around and head on back to Marysville or wherever you come from. You don't have no girlfriend or anything else here. You're in White Chalk now. I own the land you're standing on, the house she and her folks live in and she belongs to me too."

I jump between him and Bobby Joe, "If you shoot him, you're gonna have to kill me first!"

"Don't be a fool, little girl. Leave the boy here with me, so we can talk— man to man. You go on in the house."

"I won't leave him! I don't belong to you. We rent from you but we work hard to live in this rundown shack. You don't own us!" I'm crying and screaming.

My folks hear the commotion and come running out on the porch. Papa Joe and my brother Lincoln are in front. Linc has the rifle by his side. He's quiet, but he has a mean streak. Nobody messes with Linc. He works for the sawmill and lives in Sawyersville about twenty miles from White Chalk so he's not beholding to John El and he's not scared of him either.

Papa Joe walks over to John El and says quietly, "Come on in the house. We can talk about this."

Bobby gets in his car and drives off without even saying goodnight. My Christmas day is all shot to hell. I can't even go in my room and cry alone. The house is full with my sisters and brothers and children all over the place. Irene comes out and sits on the edge of the porch with me. She puts her arm around me. We sit there holding each other, not saying anything. I feel the box with my compact in it. I hold it close to my heart and think about Bobby Joe.

Later that night when the children are asleep on their pallets and Cherub is snuggled between Irene and me in the bed; we talk.

"Baby Heart, I'm sorry about what happened tonight. I wanted to meet your boyfriend," Irene says.

"Yeah. He wanted to meet y'all. That fool spoiled everything."

"Baby Heart, I know how you feel when you young and think you in love but look at me. Look what love did for me. I've got four babies, and a shiftless husband who's drunk most of the time. If it wasn't for my summer garden and Papa Joe giving us some cured meat and a chicken now and then, we would starve to death. At least you'll have a big nice house, fine clothes and never have to worry about food or workin' if you marry John El."

"Irene, I can't believe you said that. You think I should marry him for his money, even though I hate him?"

"You may grow to love him. What can that boy do for you? I

bet he live at home with his folks, can't take care of his ownself."

"We don't intend to get married or start making babies. We got it all planned. I'm going to finish school and go to college. I'm gonna be a nurse. Bobby is going to college on a football scholarship when he graduates. He only has one more year of high school. If he gets drafted, he may have to go in the army first. Then he'll go to school on the GI bill when he gets out."

"And all them years, you think he's gonna be just waitin' for you while he's in college or the army or wherever. That boy will be gone with the first pretty woman who comes along."

"Irene, you don't even know him. I'm more worried about you and that fool you're married to. I can't stand to see your eyes all swollen shut. If it hadn't been for the children, I would've hurt him this morning. Promise me you won't go back to Willie Lee."

"I don't know, Baby Heart. I have four mouths to feed."

"Irene, you just said he don't help you take care of the kids. Y'all can stay right on here in my room. If you go back to him, you'll have another baby next year and you may be blind from all the black eyes."

"You right, Baby Heart. I ain't ever goin' back to Willie Lee."

5

THE DAY AFTER CHRISTMAS —1946

Mama Lilly is stirring around in the kitchen, making breakfast and coughing. The noise wakes me up. Irene is still sleeping. When I ease out of bed, Cherub wakes up and starts crying. I sit her on the pot, and then I poke my head in the kitchen door.

"How you feeling this morning, Mama Lilly?"

"I feel better. I ain't coughing as much."

"Where's Papa Joe?"

"He had to go down to the store first thing this mornin' to meet with John El."

"About what?"

"John El left in a huff yesterday evenin'. Told yo' daddy to be down there first thing this mornin' to go over his accounts."

I feel bad. I know what's happening is because of me. But Lord, what am I supposed to do? If I let that man come to see me, he won't be satisfied until I marry him. I don't even want to talk to him. Before I marry him I'll lay my head on the railroad track and let the train run over it.

Mama Lilly, Irene, the children and I are sitting at the table almost finished with breakfast when Willie Lee comes walking in through the backdoor. His head is hanging down and he looks ashamed like an old suck-egg dog. If he had a tail, it would be tucked between his legs, I'm sure.

"Good Mornin.' How ya'll doin'? He asks.

I keep eating. The children don't look up either. Mama Lilly looks around at him, "We doin' tolerably well, Willie Lee. Come on in. Look on the stove and see if some biscuits and ham left."

"Thank you, Ma'am but I just want to speak to my wife."

Irene keeps her head down. "I don't have nothin' to say to you, Willie Lee."

"Come on, baby. I need to speak to you, private. Come on outside, please."

Irene shifts on the bench where she's sitting next to me. I know she's getting weak. If she talks to him, she'll go back home with him. It happens every time. I whisper to her, "Don't talk to him. He'll sweet talk you into coming back."

Willie Lee looks at me and bristles up. "Baby Heart, you stay out of this. This between me and my wife. You comin,' Irene? I just want to 'pologize for how I acted yesterday. I didn't have no business hittin' you"

"Willie Lee, you say that every time. Things don't get no better," Irene sniffles.

"I ain't askin' you to come back, jus' want to talk to you. Tell you how sorry I am."

"Oh, all right."

She gets up and follows him. Her eyes are still so swollen; she can barely see. She bumps into the screen door. He helps her down the steps. I can hear him sweet talking her, promising all sorts of things if she takes him back. I can't stand to listen to his lies anymore and get busy cleaning off the table and washing dishes.

A few minutes later, I look out the window and there go Irene and Willie Lee walking towards their house. They have their arms around each other like honeymooners.

"Where'd Irene go?" Mama Lilly, who had been busy keeping the children occupied, asks.

"Where do you think? Back home with Willie Lee to make another baby."

Mama Lilly shakes her head and looks sad. "That girl's weak as water. I don't know what's gonna happen to her." She ends her last sentence with a cough.

Papa Joe walks in, looking sad as a motherless child. "What happened, Papa Joe?" I ask him.

"It ain't good. I don't want to ruin the rest of yo' Christmas talkin' 'bout it."

"What did John El say?" Mama Lilly demands.

"He called in all my accounts. He say every penny I owe him got to be paid in full the day after New Years or we hafta pack up and get off his place."

Mama Lilly's eyes open wide with fear. "How much we owe?"

"Five hundert dollars, accordin' to John El's books."

"As much cotton as you been taking down to his gin, there ain't no way in hell you could owe him that much, Papa Joe."

"Watch yo' mouth, Baby Heart. No cussin'." Mama Lilly coughs.

"Do you keep records of how much you're charging and how much you pay off?" I ask.

"Baby Heart, you knows I ain't good at figurin'"

"We have to come up with a way to get us out of this mess. I'll go down to the store and go over the books with John El."

"I don't know 'bout that. If you go talkin' back at him like you done last night, he'll add on more."

"I ain't crazy, Papa Joe. I'm going to talk real nice to him. But I ain't going to let him touch me."

"I don't want you to. I ain't askin' you to pay debts you don't owe, Baby Heart. This here's my obligation."

NEW YEAR'S EVE 1946

I decide to wait 'til New Year's Eve to talk with John El. I put on my red skirt and green sweater and let my hair hang loose. I figure he may be in a good mood on New Year's Eve. Most everybody's feeling good; people are having a few drinks and promising God or themselves to be better the next year.

There's a long line of folk ahead of me when I walk into the store around four in the afternoon. John El is working on the cash register. He looks up and sees me, puts on a wide smile and says real loud, "Look who just walked in … Baby Heart Turner, the prettiest girl in White Chalk."

I don't say a word; don't even blink. I stay in the back of the line, letting people who come in later move ahead. When the last customer leaves, I stand in front of John El biting my lip.

"What can I get for you, Baby Heart?" He has a big grin on his face. I wish to God I could wipe it off with a slap up side his head.

"I need to talk to you, Mr. Murphy."

"What about?"

"About our account."

"I can't talk to you about that. That's bitniz between me and yo' daddy."

"Well, I know. But I'm worried because Papa Joe says you want us to move day after tomorrow and we don't have anywhere to go."

"Y'all don't have to leave if he pays his bill."

"Where do you think my daddy is gonna get five-hundred dollars in two days?"

"I ain't thought about it at all. I tell you what; I'm getting ready to close up in a few minutes. I got to see a man about a dog. Come on ride with me over there and we can talk about it in the car. Maybe I can come up with some kind of arrangement."

"I don't know about going somewhere with you in your car. Anyway, I got to be home before dark."

"Oh, come on. I'll have you home before dark."

"Promise you won't touch me or try to kiss me."

"You may not know it, but I'm a gentleman. I've never forced myself on a woman in my life and I ain't about to start now. There're a whole lot of women would give their right arm for a kiss from John El Murphy. Make up your mind. I got to go."

I think about Papa Joe and Mama Lilly with nowhere to live. I can go on back to town, go to school, be all comfy and warm in Miz

Miller's pretty house. But I wouldn't have one minute's peace knowing I caused my parents to be put out in the cold. I look at him and force a smile. "Okay, I'll ride with you."

The car is dark green, big with fishtail style fenders. I've never been inside a Cadillac before. It has a nice, fresh smell. I heard my brothers talking once about 'a new car smell.' I guess this is what they meant.

I settle in and begin to feel important. John El pushes a button; the windshield wipers come on. He pushes another button and water sprays on the windshield. I ain't never seen anything like this before in my life. I don't want him to know I'm beginning to feel good about riding in his new car. So I frown instead of smile.

I clear my throat and say, "I'm ready to talk."

"How you like this car, Baby Heart?"

"It's real nice, Mr. Murphy. But I want to talk about how we can settle my daddy's debt."

"You can stop calling me Mr. Murphy. Just call me John El." He reaches over and pats my knee. I push his hand away and move as close to the door as I can get without falling out.

"Well, John El, could you see your way clear to let my parents stay on 'til spring or lower the bill so Papa Joe can pay it off?"

"That depends on how nice you gonna be to me."

"What do you mean?" My heart is pumping fast. I'm afraid of what he's going to say or do next.

"I mean get rid of the boyfriend and let me come callin' on you."

I grit my teeth. The thought of losing Bobby Joe for the likes of John El Murphy causes my stomach to knot. I have no intention of doing what he asked but decide to play it cool so I can make a deal with him.

"I don't mind you coming to visit, but I'll be back in school day after tomorrow."

"I can drive to Marysville to see you."

"Oh, no." I shake my head. "I mean I have homework and I work at the beauty shop…no time for courting."

He turns his head to look at me. "I bet you got plenty time for that boy who followed you all the way to White Chalk."

I keep my mouth shut for a while, trying to think what I should say next. I don't want to offend him. "Well, you can come by tonight." I look up and we're entering the city limits of Marysville. "You didn't tell me you were going to Marysville."

"I thought you might want to see your boyfriend," he says with a sly grin.

As we approach the residential section of town where colored folks live I crouch down, hoping no one will see me. Then I recognize that he's turning onto Miz Miller's street. I'm scared to death Bobby Joe may see us. "Where're we going? I thought you had to see a man about a dog."

"That's just a figure of speech. But I do hope to see a dog. Actually he's more like a puppy tryin' to piss in a big dog's territory. I hear his name is Bobby Joe Miller and you live with his aunt."

Jimmy, a classmate of Bobby's, is walking down the street. John El blows the horn and beckons to the boy. He comes over. John El rolls down the window and asks him, "Where can I find Bobby Joe Miller?"

Maybe Jimmy sees me shaking my head. He says, "I think he went out of town."

"Where he live?"

"Why don't you ask Baby Heart? She's his girlfriend," the boy says and walks away.

If looks could kill, I'd be dead from the daggers shooting from John El's eyes.

"She was his girlfriend! She's mine now!" John El yells as he rolls the window up and guns the motor.

When we're back on the road to White Chalk, he asks me, "Have you had anything to do with that boy?"

"I don't know what you're talking about," I say.

He looks at me with that hard, squinty mean look of his. "You know damned well what I mean. Have you ever let him do it to you?"

I don't say anything for a while. I think about lying. Maybe if I say "yes" he will leave me alone. But if I do, I know for sure it won't help my family. I whisper, "No."

"Keep it that way. Remember, you belong to me now. You gonna be my wife. John El Murphy don't take no damaged goods."

I hang my head and don't dispute him. "What about my parents?"

"As long as you're my girl, yo' family's debt is forgiven."

"We will pay you. We just need more time. And maybe you can reduce it some?"

"I'll cut it in half. Tell your daddy I changed it to two-hundred-fifty dollars and he's got until spring."

"Thank you, Mr. Murphy ... I mean John El."

"I won't be over tonight. Got other plans. But you remember one thing — John El Murphy always gets what he wants. You **will** be my wife. And you better come to me pure."

7

JANUARY 1947

Candy and I sway as Lincoln's old car rattles along the rough country roads. Linc is driving us back to Marysville on New Years Day so we will be ready for school tomorrow.

On the way, I talk to him about Papa Joe's debt to John El. Linc asks me, "How much Papa Joe, owe?"

"At first John El said it was five-hundred dollars. I got him to cut it in half."

Linc shoots me a suspicious look. "How'd you do that?"

"I just talked nice to him and asked if he could see fit to reduce it. I don't think Papa Joe really owed him that much in the first place. He was going to make them move tomorrow. He says they can stay on if it's paid up by spring."

The big vein in Linc's temple is throbbing. It does that when he gets mad.

"I'll take care of it." He tells me. "And don't you let that dog touch you. If he tries somethin', tell me. Everybody else may be scared of him but I'll blow his head off while he's reachin' for that popgun he carries if he tries to hurt you."

"I don't want you getting in trouble, Linc. I've caused enough problems already."

"This ain't yo' fault, Baby Heart. He's got no business saying who you can be with and he sure as hell don't own you or anybody else in my family. Slavery ended a long time ago."

Candy sits in the back listening but she doesn't say anything. I haven't had a chance to tell her what happened since I was over to her house with Bobby Joe on Christmas day. I feel my burdens lightening after I talk to Linc. I look out the car window, watching the evergreen trees run by like they did when I was a little girl. Back then I thought the trees were running instead of the car.

I'm happy when we get close to Marysville because my heart is there. It's there with Bobby Joe.

I'm up at dawn getting ready for school. I can't wait to see Bobby Joe. I leave ahead of Candy and get to school before most of the teachers. I stand outside looking for him.

When I see him coming down the street, my heart shudders and skips. I run to meet him. I want to hug him, but he has one arm full of books and so do I. My free arm finds its way around his waist. He pushes it away. I look in his eyes. They're filled with something I've never seen before. They're no longer soft and loving. Is it hate I see? Is it anger? Is it scorn? I can take the anger, even hate though I did nothing to deserve it. But scorn —I can't take scorn.

"Bobby Joe, what's wrong?"

"As if you don't know."

"Don't know what?"

"Get away from me, Jolee."

"Bobby, is it because of John El Murphy?"

"I guess it wasn't bad enough that he threatened my life when I came to White Chalk. You had to ride into town in his new car so all of my friends could see you with him."

"Bobby Joe, I love you! Please let me explain" I reach out my hand to touch him.

"Stay away from me, Jolee Turner, and take your love with you." He walks away fast—leaving me behind — leaving a hurting in my heart.

Before today I only knew the sweet part of love. Now love tastes rough and bitter like a persimmon peel in my mouth; causing a pain that hurts so bad, I almost faint.

I'm sitting right in front of Miz Robinson, my math teacher. I don't know how long she's been calling my name. She walks over to my desk and shakes me by the shoulder. "Jolee Turner, what's wrong with you? Are you in a trance? I've called on you twice to go to the board." She feels my forehead. "Are you sick?"

"Yes, Ma'am. I don't feel good."

"Maybe you're coming down with the flu. Do you want to go home?"

"Yes, Ma'am."

"Do you want Candy to walk home with you?"

"No, Ma'am. I can make it home by myself."

The other kids look at me like they know something is wrong and it's not the flu. I think they've been talking about me behind my back. About me being seen with a grown man, old enough to be my daddy. My heart is hurting and I'm ashamed. I gather my books, and slink out of the classroom feeling lower than a snake's underside.

Miz Miller is at home when I get there. The beauty parlor is closed on Mondays. She hears me come in and meets me in the living room. "Baby Heart, why are you home so early?"

"I'm not feeling good. The teacher sent me home."

"Where're you hurting?" Miz Miller's eyes are warm and concerned, reminding me of my mother.

"All over. I'm aching everywhere."

"Go to bed, Baby Heart. I'll make some soup. If you don't feel better, I'll call the doctor."

I crawl into bed and pull the wool blanket and pink chenille bedspread tight around my body. I want to tell her no doctor can heal what's hurting me. My heart is breaking. Can a doctor fix that? Can he make me stop loving Bobby Joe? John El Murphy is ruining my life. Can a doctor make him leave me alone? He said he always gets what he wants. Lord/God, I pray, don't let him get me.

Candy comes in our room after school and throws her books on the floor. She plops down on the bed beside me. "Baby Heart, what's the matter?"

"Don't you know? I'm sure you've heard everybody talking about it. Bobby Joe quit me because of John El."

"I didn't know what happened until today. I tried to talk to Bobby. I tried to tell him that you don't want John El. But he wouldn't listen."

I turn my face to the wall and don't say anymore. I stay like that for three days. On the third day Miz Miller comes in and says, "Baby Heart, you're not the first girl had her heart broken by a boy. I've been through the same thing. Tell me what happened."

Before I know it, I'm telling her everything through sobs and a flood of tears.

"Don't worry, Baby Heart. I'm calling that nephew of mine. I'll get him over here and make him listen. That boy's crazy in love with you. He's just embarrassed and too young and silly to know what to do with his feelings. I bet he's hurting just as bad as you…" She looks back at me with a smile on her pretty face as she heads for the phone. "Get out of that bed and fix yourself up before he gets here."

When I hear the doorbell ring, my heart starts racing. I push the hair back off my damp forehead. I feel giddy like I might faint. What if he looks at me with scorn in his eyes? I'm afraid to go out there. Miz Miller pokes her head in my bedroom door. "Bobby Joe is here to see you, Baby Heart." Her voice sounds sweet like a melody.

"I don't want to see him."

"Yes you do. If you didn't want to see him why did you get all prettied up in that yellow skirt and navy blue sweater? I smell Evening in Paris perfume. Looks to me like you want to see him as bad as he wants to see you."

"Did he say he wants to see me?"

"He came over here to see you, Baby Heart. Now come on out here before I get me a switch to your behind," she says playfully with a twinkle in her eyes. "I can't stand your lovesick moping and staying in bed any longer."

He gets up from the sofa when I enter the living room. "Hey, Baby Heart," he says, while stuffing his hands in his pockets like he doesn't know what to do with them. He studies the floor. I think he's afraid to look me in the eye.

"Hey, Bobby Joe." I stand still, afraid to move closer to him; afraid he will push me away. We've never been shy like this around each other before. It's a strange feeling because we're not strangers. But how do we get back to where we were before our hearts were shattered?

Miz Miller is standing there watching us. She comes to the rescue. "Bobby Joe Miller, can't you see that this girl loves you just like you love her?"

"I hope she does, Aunt Trudy. But after what I heard, it's hard to believe."

"Baby Heart, tell Bobby Joe what happened, just like you told me. Bobby, I want you to listen not just with your ears but with your heart."

I hesitate. I don't like telling Bobby Joe that my parents own nothing, would have likely been put out if I hadn't gone for that ride with John El. I decide it's better to lose some pride than Bobby Joe.

Biting my lower lip, I plunge in. "John El claims he's been liking me since I was a baby. He got my daddy's permission to come courting when I turned fifteen. When Papa Joe told me about his agreement with John El, I flat out refused to keep company with him. It wasn't a problem with me being in Marysville — until Christmas. I didn't know he was coming to see me Christmas day. I'm so sorry you got caught up in that."

"I don't understand, Baby Heart. What kind of grown man sees a baby and wants her for a girlfriend?"

"A strange one I guess."

"That still doesn't explain why you were riding around Marysville with him." A hint of anger mixes with the hurt in his voice.

"After you left Christmas night, he was angry as a mad dog. He told my daddy to meet him at his store the next morning. He called in Papa Joe's debt — five hundred dollars worth. That may not sound like much money to most folks but it's the same as asking for the moon or stars from poor folks like us."

I look at Bobby Joe and notice his face begin to soften and his eyes become moist.

"He gave my daddy until the third of January to either pay up or get off his property. I knew it was because of me. I went to his store to see if I could get him to back off. I didn't want to get in the car with him but I didn't want my folks out in the cold, either. He promised he wouldn't touch me and he didn't."

"Why did you come to Marysville and ride down streets where my friends or I could see you?"

"I swear I didn't know he was coming to Marysville. That was a trick intended to break us up and it looks like it worked." Out of the corner of my eye, I see Miz Miller tiptoe out of the room, leaving us alone.

Bobby Joe moves closer and puts his arms around me. "Baby Heart, I'm sorry. I'll understand if you don't want to be my girlfriend anymore. I was embarrassed, jealous and hurt when Jimmy told me he saw you with that man. That's no excuse for the way I acted. I should have talked to you, heard your side."

I snuggle close to him and lay my head on his shoulder. I feel my heart knitting back together. "Bobby Joe, I love you. We belong with each other. I want to be your girl."

"What if he comes after you?"

"My brother Lincoln is handling everything. He's going to settle the debt and make sure John El leaves me alone."

I strut into my classroom the next day —head high, heart striking a strong, steady beat. Bobby Joe is back by my side. I'm happy in love again — so satisfied.

EASTER 1947

Spring crept through the winter drabness as soft and easy as a crawling baby. I look around one day and flowers are pushing their heads up though the warm Georgia soil. I watch blue jays; sparrows and all kinds of birds fly overhead together in staggered groups each with their own kind. They're singing sweet love songs. I can tell they're happy to be with their mates gliding above in the warm spring breezes. I feel free and happy as one of those birds.

Bobby Joe and I are together every chance we get. We talk about our future. He wants to go to college and major in physical education so he can coach football. I still want to be a nurse. I picture myself in a white uniform topped off by the nurse's crisp white hat trimmed in black. Long black hair flows down my back from underneath it. My white shoes are spotless. I stick a thermometer under a patient's tongue, frown when I take it out and have to tell her she's running a temperature.

Whether Bobby Joe and I daydream together or alone, we know we'll be together forever. He plans to go to Morehouse or Morris Brown College. I will go to Grady School of Nursing. They're all located in Atlanta. We can still see each other. There is no dream awake or sleeping without Bobby Joe in it. We don't know how we'll pay for college but we've heard of students working their way through school and Bobby Joe may get a football scholarship.

He'll finish high school two years before me, but I'm not worried about some other girl in Atlanta turning his head. I know his heart is true. He's mine. And I'm his. We'll get married after college. He doesn't need to ask because we believe that will happen as surely as we breathe.

Now that Lincoln has a car, Mama Lilly and Papa Joe don't have to come to town in the wagon any more. They stop by the beauty shop to see me every Saturday. Today is the Saturday before Easter and I'm real busy washing hair and making money. Linc's car pulls up in front of the beauty shop window. I wrap my customer's hair in a towel and tell her I'll be right back.

I run outside to the car and lean into the passenger's side where Mamma Lilly is sitting and give her a kiss. Papa Joe is in the back. Mama Lilly starts coughing and it looks like she's never gonna stop. She motions for me to move back so she can open the door. She leans out and releases a mouthful of white frothy stuff to the pavement.

I don't like this one bit. I look at Linc and Papa Joe with unspoken questions in my eyes. Linc shakes his head slowly and Papa Joe looks straight ahead, real worried like. Then he asks, "Baby Heart, ain't you comin' home for Easter?"

"Yes, Sir, if Linc can come and get me tomorrow. I'll get ready for church and be home for dinner afterwards."

Lincoln smiles and says, I'll pick you up at nine in the mornin'."

I watch the car as they pull off with an uneasy feeling.

Easter Sunday morning finds me up early. I put on the new baby blue rayon suit and white pumps that I bought with some of the money I made at the beauty shop. As I admire myself in the mirror, I feel a little sad that Bobby Joe won't see me in my new outfit. I wish I could be with him today but I need to be with my folks.

I haven't been home since Christmas — mainly because I work on Friday evenings and Saturdays. Linc offered to pick me up some Sunday mornings and bring me back Sunday evening but I always beg off sayin' I have homework. I'm scared to go back to White Chalk — scared John El may come callin', come to collect his debt.

Easter Sunday morning is beautiful. There's not a cloud in the sky — all blue. Birds are singing. Easter Lillie's are in bloom. The little kids who live on either side of Miz Miller are out on their front lawn. They're all excited about an Easter egg hunt and the chocolate Easter bunnies they couldn't wait to bite the ears off before they left for Sunday school.

I have an Easter basket filled with eggs I colored last night. I'm taking them with me for Irene's children. I have a special bunny for my little Cherub. I rush to the curb with my arms full as soon as I see his car. Linc jumps out and helps me put my stuff in the back. "Happy Easter, Linc."

"Happy Easter, little sister. You sure look pretty. All my sisters good-lookin' but you the prettiest."

On the way to White Chalk, Linc and I talk. "Have ya'll paid John El?" I ask.

"Yeah. I paid him every red cent of what he claim Papa Joe owed him. Then he had the nerve to start talkin' 'bout interes'. I laid my Smith and Wesson on his counter with my finger on the trigger and tole him, this the only interes' you gonna git."

"He might try to collect the interest from Papa Joe or hold it over our heads some other way," I say, worry edging into my voice.

"He backed off. Papa Joe was with me. I tole Papa Joe right then an' there, no more runnin' credit with John El. Anything you need, I'll take you to town to buy."

"I bet John El didn't like that."

"I suppose not. But there ain't nothin' he kin do 'bout it. I wrote Roosevelt. Between the two of us, we hopin' to git Papa Joe and Mama Lilly away frum White Chalk. Hope to sit him down so he won't have to share crop no mo'. He'll be 65 in a year, eligible for his old age pension."

"I didn't know Papa Joe's that old."

"He's a old man. You're the baby. Roosevelt, the oldest one of us, is goin' on forty-five. I been thinkin' of goin' to Boston to live near Roosevelt. Maybe gettin' us all outta White Chalk."

I listen to what Lincoln's saying with mixed feelings. Getting away from White Chalk, a long ways from John El Murphy, would be a good thing for my family and me. But I shudder at the thought of moving up North to some cold, snowy city far away from Bobby Joe.

"That may not be a bad idea as long as I can stay here in Marysville and finish high school. I'm worried about Mama Lilly. That cough is getting worse."

"I know. We take her to the doctor every Saturday but the medicine ain't doin' no good. I was hopin' if we git her away frum all this white dust her lungs may clear up. But it may be too late."

"What do you mean, 'too late'?"

"I don't want to spoil yo' Easter Sunday. But the doctor is talkin' 'bout operatin' on her. You betta talk to Papa Joe."

"Are they coming to church?"

"Yeah. One of the others will pick them up."

Rose of Sharon Baptist Church comes in to view. Rose of Sharon is the same as being home. It's my home church. I can't remember when I first came here — probably when I was a baby. The small white church has a steeple. Dust from the chalk mine keeps it looking freshly painted.

We arrive before the service starts. People are gathering in front, eager to talk to each other. Friends and relatives greet me with a hug, happy to see me. Miz Sadie walks over to me wearing a big red straw hat with a bird perched in a nest on top of it. She smiles and a gold tooth flashes. "We so proud of you, Baby Heart. We finally gonna have a girl frum White Chalk finish high school. I hear you gonna be a nurse."

"Yes, Ma'am. I want to be a nurse but that's a long ways off. I got three more years of high school and then I'll have to go to college four years."

"Just take it a day at a time, sugar. You'll be surprised how fast them years go by."

The ladies all have on big straw hats with flowers or feathery plumes shooting off in all directions. Some of the hats have fruit of all kinds on top. Veils cover some faces; others are wide-open showing off broad Easter smiles. The women around me look like a flower garden, many different skin colors — ranging from jet black to high yellow— all wearing their colorful Easter finery.

No matter how poor they are, all the ladies who attend Rose of Sharon wear hats and have at least one silk dress of a bright color to wear to church on Sundays. They all have one black dress to wear to funerals. And the men have a suit and tie. The seat of their pants may be shiny from wear but they know how to give proper respect to the Lord when they meet in His house by wearing their best clothes. I like that about my church.

Papa Joe and Mama Lilly arrive late with my sister Rose and her children. They sit across the aisle from Linc and me. I look around for Irene but I'm not surprised that she and her kids didn't come. Children go up to the pulpit wearing new clothes and recite Easter speeches about the Risen Savior.

Little Georgia Reeves is dressed to kill in a pink organdy dress with puff sleeves and pretty blue glass buttons. Long bouncy curls hang from underneath her pink Easter bonnet. Her brother, Stanley about six, takes the stage with her and they say their speech together in singsong rhymes. I can tell they're proud of themselves when they march back down the isle to the sound of applause from the congregation.

I feel sad because Irene's kids don't have new Easter outfits. I know that's why they're not in church. I promise myself that I will save enough money next year to buy every one of them new clothes even if I have to wear the same suit again.

Quite a few of the members are coughing so loud they sound like a chorus. They begin to drown out the choir and the children's Easter speeches. Mama Lilly is part of the cough chorus, so she isn't so noticeable at first. But the others calm down and she keeps going until she's almost in convulsions.

Papa Joe puts his arm around her and helps her outside. I get up and follow them. Mama Lilly is spitting up the frothy white stuff, streaked with blood again. I put my arms around her. Her forehead is beaded with cold clammy sweat.

Damn John El Murphy and his chalk mine! He's killing half the people around here. I keep this thought to myself. It wouldn't do to cuss in the churchyard or in hearing of Mama Lilly, especially on Easter Sunday.

"Mama Lilly needs help, Papa Joe. What're we gonna do?" I ask him.

Papa Joe ushers me out of her earshot and speaks in a whisper, "I talked to the doctor, Baby Heart. She needs to go to a hospital in Atlanta. Doctor Scott say one of her lungs got cancer. If they don't get it out soon, the cancer's gonna spread to the other one."

"How long we got, Papa Joe?"

"The doctor say if they don't operate soon, she'll be gone in six months."

"What're we waiting for? You and Linc have to get her to Atlanta tomorrow."

"Well, it ain't that easy, Baby Heart. We need money for a operation."

"I always thought if people are real sick and don't have money to go to the hospital or pay for the operation, the doctors just take care of them."

"Na, Baby Heart. Country folks like us fill Dr. Scott's office with vegetables, ham an' eggs 'cause we don't have money. But big city doctors don't take rations. Only hard cold cash."

"How much money we need, Papa Joe?"

"Over a thousand dollars."

"We can't just let Mama Lilly die. Maybe we can borrow the money."

"Yo' brothers already tried that. The people at the bank say we don't have no collateral — whatever that is. I don't know what do 'cept pray." He looks so worn and helpless in his one shoddy suit and necktie that he relies on Mama Lilly to tie for him. I know Papa Joe won't last long without her. And I can't bear to lose my parents. My heart and head both ache with the thought of losing them.

I only know one man who's got that kind of money. My worse fears take the form of a green-eyed devil with a pointed tail and pitchfork dancing around gleefully in my mind's eye. I was afraid John El would come calling on me. Now it seems like I'm the one who'll be looking for him.

Easter Sunday started out so beautiful. Now my world is crashing in on me. I look to the sky and see clouds gathering, white fluffy ones. But I know it won't be long before they turn dark, real dark and stormy.

SPRING BREAK —1947

School is closed the whole week after Easter for Spring Break. I stay on in the country with my folks. My heart is heavy and my head is full of bad thoughts about what I have to do. I want to talk to somebody first. I can't tell Lincoln. I know he won't allow me to sacrifice my life for Mama's as much as he loves her. I have to be careful. I don't want him to find out what I'm thinking about doing.

I consider telling Irene but she has enough trouble of her own. She showed up at our sister Rose's for dinner with the family on Easter Sunday. Her front tooth was out. It seems Willie Lee stopped blackening her eyes and started knocking out her teeth. The children were dirty and hungry. My happiest moment was watching little Cherub's eyes light up when she saw the cuddly, pink Easter bunny I gave her. She didn't let that bunny out of her sight the rest of the day.

Irene is showing — pregnant again; just like I predicted the day after Christmas when she went back to Willie Lee with her arm all around his waist as they walked home together. No point talking to Irene. She already told me I should marry a rich man. Better to get knocked up and knocked around by a rich one than a poor one is her motto. She doesn't know how sweet men can be, even though she should. Papa Joe's always been good to Mama Lilly and all us kids.

Candy is home. I decide to talk to her. Not being a part of my family, maybe she can help me see what I should do. Easter Monday afternoon, I walk over to Candy's. We're sitting in her front porch swing, moving back and forth in a slow steady motion, when she says, "A penny for your thoughts, Baby Heart. You're so quiet today."

"You just wasted a penny, Candy. You know who I'm always thinking about."

"Yeah. Bobby Joe. But why are you looking so sad? I can usually tell when you're thinking about him, 'cause you're smiling and laughing to yourself."

"Today is different. I'm sad because I have to quit him."

"Why?!

"You heard me. I have to."

"Have you lost your mind? You love that boy and he loves you. It's like you two were made for each other."

"What would you do, Candy, if your mother was going to die but you had the power to save her life?"

"I would save her life," Candy says simply, pumping the swing a little faster.

"Even if it meant giving up the boy you love?"

"I don't know. I mean I've never been in love. I like Eugene but I'm not in love with him. If it came to saving my mother or losing him, I wouldn't think twice about what to do."

"You answered my question. I would be a selfish, heartless person to let my mother die."

"Is Miz Lilly sick?"

"Yeah. She's got to have an operation or she's gonna die. Problem is we don't have money. I believe John El will pay for it if I agree to marry him."

Candy looks at me, her eyes wide and filled with tears. "Oh, Baby Heart!" Then she hugs me tight — her hug is real strong, it feels like the air is being squeezed out of my lungs. Maybe she thinks if she hugs me hard and long enough she can make all my troubles go away.

The next day, I put on my pretty yellow sun-back dress and walk down to John El's store. The man working behind the counter tells me, "He's not here. He's at the chalk mine."

I have to talk to him now, while I have my nerve and courage up. What I have to do feels like taking castor oil when I have a bad cold. Dreading it is the hardest part. Taking castor oil is the nastiest tasting, most gosh-awful thing I've ever done. I learned that you have to just plunge ahead and swallow it fast while you hold your nose.

This is gonna be worse. There will be no slice of orange or piece of hard rock candy to take away the bad taste afterwards. And this castor oil won't go away after one swallow. I'll have to take it every day for the rest of my life. But if I don't, Mama Lilly will have no life.

I've only been to the chalk mine once before. I waited outside that day while Papa Joe went in to look for my brother. Today my knees are trembling. I want to turn around and run back home. But I speed up instead. The April sun is warm and I'm sweating.

Big strong logs hold up slabs of chalk at the top of the mine. The entranceway looks like a large mouth gapping wide open. Two lights far back in the big mouth could be tonsils but are more like cat eyes glowing in the dark; a big cat crouching to pounce on a mouse. I think that cat is John El and I'm the mouse he's gonna pounce on.

I force myself to enter the mine even though I feel faint. It's dark and cool inside. The thick white walls are chalk and the cat eyes are lanterns hung on either side of the walls to guide the workers.

I walk further into the mine, and then I see a man coming toward me with a lantern light attached to his hardhat. He's covered with chalk from head to toe. He looks like a ghost. A white mask covers his mouth. He hollers at me. The echo from his muffled voice bounces off the chalk walls, scattering white dust in front of him.

"Hey! Where you goin'? You can't come in here. Only workers allowed inside the mine."

I holler back. "I gotta see Mr. Murphy. It's an emergency."

"Mr. Murphy busy. He got inspectors here today. You want me to give him a message?"

"Yes, Sir. Tell him Baby Heart needs to talk to him."

I walk home with a downcast spirit inside me. I wish I could have just got it over with one way or the other. Maybe he would have laughed at me and said he was only kidding, that he never wanted to marry me but he would gladly pay for Mama Lilly's operation seeing as how her condition was probably caused by his mine. I know that's too much to hope for.

On the other hand, he might just squint his green eyes and say he's not going to spend no money on a Turner, period. If he says that, I will feel like I did all I could to save Mama Lilly and I can be at peace and still have Bobby Joe. I don't know what to do with all these thoughts churning around in my head. I wish I could talk to Miz Miller. She could calm me down. But we don't have a phone and she's in Marysville.

I'm sitting on my front porch later on this evening. It's almost dark. I hear the humming of the motor first and then the sleek, dark-green Cadillac comes into view. It turns onto the road leading to my house. My heart is thudding in my chest. Every time it jumps, I want to run and hide. I want to cry out for Bobby Joe. Instead, I sit still with my head down.

I hear the car door open and slam shut. His boots make a clopping sound each time they land on the old worn wooden steps to the front porch. I just sit there, real still with my head bowed, hoping all of this is a bad dream: Mama Lilly isn't dying, John El isn't standing in front of me and I'm not about to lose Bobby Joe.

His voice rings out. I can't pretend I'm dreaming anymore. This is real.

"Is this the way you greet company, Miz Jolee Turner?"

"How you mean?"

"I mean you sent word you wanted to see me. Now you sit here with yo' head down and won't even look at me. I don't have time to play games, girl." His voice is sharp like the cutting edge of a razor.

I look up at him. He's clean, hair slicked back with some kind of pomade. He smells like Old Spice after-shave lotion. He's wearing brown slacks with a red-checkered short-sleeved shirt that makes him look like a country hick. That's what he is. So I suppose it's the natural look for him. It's clear he dressed up to come courting. I swallow hard and decide it's time to take my dose of castor oil.

"Good evening, Mr. Murphy, I mean John El. How you feeling?"

His face is twisted between a smile and a sneer. "I'm feeling fine. What do you want to see me about? My worker said it was some kind of emergency."

"It is. Have a seat." I pat the bench I'm sitting on for him to sit beside me.

He sits much closer than I intend. His leg presses against mine. And the rest of his body is so close to me I can't slide a pin between us if I tried. I move over a little so I can breathe. He lights a cigarette and offers me one.

I shake my head. "No, Sir. I don't smoke. I wanted to see you about my mother."

A look of curiosity crosses his face. "What about your mother?"

"She's real sick, John El. The doctor says she's going to die if she don't have a operation soon." My eyes cloud up and tears start rolling. I'm not a crybaby. But I feel like crying today. Maybe a few tears will soften him up. So I let them flow.

He looks puzzled. "Gee whiz. I'm sorry to hear about Miz Lilly. But I still don't know why you sent for me. I'm not exactly considered family or close friend by the Turners." His words come out in a slow drawl.

"John El, you know we don't have money for no operation. I was hoping you could see your way clear …"

"You got to be kiddin'. After the way you and your family treated me. You batted yo' eyelashes and I cut yo' daddy's debt in half. Then your brother, Lincoln, threatened my life and refused to pay interest on all the bills Joe owed. Now I suppose you think you can bat yo' eyelashes, cry a little bit and I'm gonna pay for yo' mama's operation.

"Little girl, I like you but John El Murphy ain't nobody's fool. Before you ask me to pay for yo' mama's operation, I need to know what you puttin' up for collateral?"

"John El, I don't know what that is."

"Collateral is somethin' of equal value. For instance, if the operation costs ten thousand dollars, then you got to let me hold something of yours worth that amount."

"John El, if I had something worth ten thousand dollars I wouldn't be asking you to loan us money."

"Well then, I'm sorry. But I can't hand out hard cold cash without something to secure the debt. I'm a bitniz man not a social worker." He gets up and starts down the steps.

I have to bargain myself off quick before I lose my nerve or he leaves. I stand up with my eyes closed, dig my fingernails into my arms and ask, "Can I be collateral?"

He turns around, walks over, faces me and holds me by my arms while he looks into my eyes. Corn liquor on his breath mixes with the aftershave lotion he's wearing causing a sickening sweetish smell. "That depends on how you mean. If you talkin' 'bout a quick screw for that kind of money — no way. But if you sayin' you'll marry me, I'll consider it."

"I'll marry you," I whisper.

"Set the date for the weddin' and spread the word we're getting married. I want everybody to know you're promised to me."

"Yes, Sir. There's only one thing."

"What's that?"

"Can I at least finish out this year in school before I marry you? It's only a little over a month until school closes for the summer."

He raises one eyebrow, "Can't stand to leave that boyfriend you got over in Marysville?"

"No, Sir. That's not it. I just want to finish out the school year. I would like to continue goin' to school after we marry. I want to be a nurse."

"I'll think about lettin' you finish out this year. But the only nurse you gonna be is to our babies. A wife's place is at home. I can take care of you in style. You ain't never got to empty no bedpans and walk floors takin' care of sick folks. You're the luckiest colored gal in Georgia. You're gonna have maids waitin' on you, Baby Heart."

He has no idea what I'm feeling — how much I want to take care of the sick and how proud it would make me feel. I think twice before I speak again. The only sick person I need to save right now is Mama Lilly. "All right. I'll spread the word. But we don't have no money for a wedding if that's what you got in mind."

He pulls my long ponytail over one shoulder and winds it around his hand. "Don't worry yo' pretty little head about that. Find somebody who plans big weddins. Tell her what you want. Don't spare no expense. John El Murphy and his new bride gonna have the biggest weddin' colored folks and most whites ever seen in these parts. There's just one thing you need to know, Baby Heart."

My eyes are closed. I can't bear to look in his mean old watery green eyes. All I can think about is Bobby Joe, his eyes so kind and brown. And how I'm going to break his heart. "What?" I ask John EL.

"Don't get the idea you can play me. If you even think about runnin' out on yo' promise, I'll shoot you dead. If I can't find you, anybody in yo' family will do." He pats the gun on his hip. "One more thing. I don't take damaged goods. If you been foolin' around with that boy in Marysville, you better tell me now and we can call the whole thing off."

I stand before him with bowed head and shudder. "No, Sir. I'm still a virgin."

"Make sure you keep it that way. I'll find out on our weddin' night if you're lyin' to me."

"Don't you want to find out before we get married?" I hold my breath.

"I tole you, I ain't no fool. If I open the door what would stop him from goin' in? No, thank you. I'll wait."

"You gonna ask my daddy for my hand?"

"Tomorrow. After I get all the information about the hospital expenses. I plan to visit Doctor Scott myself."

"Don't tell Papa Joe I asked about you paying Mama Lilly's hospital bill. If he knows about that, he may not consent."

"Thanks for the tip."

He turns and walks away without even saying goodnight. It's just a business deal to him. He's buying me same as he buys a prize horse he's always wanted. I sit alone on the porch sobbing my eyes out while the whip-poor-wills sing their sad song in the gathering darkness of night.

I creep quietly into Mama Lilly's room before day the next morning. She's pale and thin as a reed beneath the white sheet. Papa Joe is sound asleep beside her. He's snoring softly. I watch and listen to the wet gurgling sound as she struggles for breath. I'm doing the right thing. If my sacrifice can give her a few more years free from suffering it will be worth it.

I think about the holy man in the bible who was going to sacrifice his son as a burned offering to God. I can't remember which one he was. But I know how he felt when he was about to lay his child on the fire. As I recall, God hid a ram in the bushes and accepted it as an offering instead of the son.

I wonder if He has a surprise in store for me. Maybe He will prepare a beautiful woman for John El, one he can't resist. We can pay the money he loans us for the operation back on the installment plan. Mama Lilly will get well and I can go back to school and Bobby Joe.

I bow my head and move my lips silently in prayer, *Lord, I pray you will see your way clear to prepare another offering to take my place with John El. If you don't, I understand and pray that my sacrifice will save Mama Lilly's life and be acceptable in your sight. Amen.*

10

TAKE MY HAND

I love to watch sunsets.

This evening the sun spreads in golden orange flames before it flattens out over the horizon with lavender colored ribbons along the edge. The lavender is new to me. I don't recall seeing these lavender colors before. Maybe God is sending me a sign.

Dusk gathers slowly. Papa Joe is out back feeding the chickens before they go into the henhouse to roost for the night. I've freshened myself up and combed my hair. It hangs in long braids over each shoulder.

I hear a car humming in the distance. My stomach churns as the sound of the car comes closer. I want to run and hide. Instead I walk around the house and sit down on the edge of the front porch. I calm myself down by inhaling the scent of the sweet magnolia blossoms near the porch and watch him get out of the car and walk to where I'm sitting.

John El is grinning. "Good Evenin,' Baby Heart. Is Big Joe around?"

"He's in the back yard feeding the chickens." I keep looking at the ground, hoping it will open up and swallow me.

"You lookin' mighty pretty." He takes one of my braids and winds it around his hand. "You got the prettiest hair I ever seen. I been watchin' it grow since you was a baby. Been wantin' to feel it since then. Now it's gonna be all mine." The creepy look in his eyes sends a cold chill through my body.

I shiver while I watch him strut off. His western boots with spurs in the back, kick up dust as he goes to find Papa Joe. About the same time, a red bantam rooster struts across the yard, his feathers ruffled, on his way to the feed pan. I laugh at the resemblance between the rooster and John El.

I hear them talking low for a few minutes. I can't make out their words but I know he's asking for my hand in marriage. Finally they walk over to where I'm sitting on the front porch clutching the edge so tight, my knuckles look white.

Papa Joe says, "Baby Heart, John El here done asked for yo' hand in marriage. Come along with me. I wanna talk to you in private before I give him my answer."

Papa Joe takes my hand and leads me behind the house. He stops and looks up at the sky for a minute before he speaks.

"Baby Heart, tell me the truth. Do you want to marry him?"

I've never lied to Papa Joe before but I have to today. I bite my bottom lip and say, "Yes Sir."

"I thought you wanted to finish school. He ain't gonna let you go back to school after you git married."

"I know. But he can give me a lot more than I can make being a nurse, waiting on sick folks. I thought about what you said last summer, about him being able to take care of me in style. I made up my mind, Papa Joe. Better to be an old man's darling than a young man's fool. Right?"

"I don't know about that, Baby Heart. I just want you to be happy."

Papa Joe studies my face for a long time before he asks, "You sho this ain't got nothin' to do with us needin' money to pay for Lilly's operation?"

"No, Sir. It ain't got nothing to do with that."

"If you sho this is what you want, I'll give him yo' hand."

Papa Joe and I walk back to where he's sitting on the edge of the porch smoking a cigarette. "John El, I'm givin' you my daughter's hand in marriage. I 'spec you to take good care of her. I done already raised her, so I ain't toleratin' no beatin' on her. If you can't git along, bring her back where you got her frum."

"You don't need to worry about that Papa Joe. I don't beat women. I'm gonna be real good to this little girl. I've been in love with her since she was big enough to toddle inside my store. Well, back then it was Mr. Scott's store."

I can't believe how easy he changed from 'Big Joe' to 'Papa Joe' and how his eyes seem to be shining with happiness. I begin to see another side of John El. Maybe he just wants a family. He doesn't have friends. His Mama's dead. His white father, Mr. Scott, couldn't own him in public. I don't know what kind of daddy he was to him. But I bet a daddy who couldn't be seen with him in the open made him feel ashamed or bad, even if he did leave all of his money and property to him.

Even though I begin to feel a little sorry for John El, the pain of losing Bobby Joe is still aching in my heart. I'm thinking all this when I hear him say to Papa Joe, "How is Miz Lilly?"

"She ain't doin' well at all, John El. Doctor say only chance to save her is a operation."

John El looks surprised. "Well, is she willing to go under the knife?"

"Yeah. We both willin' but we don't have the money."

"She's gonna be my mother in-law soon. I'll take care of it."

Papa Joe lets out a loud, "Thank you, Lawd" as he turns his face toward the sky.

"I'd like to pay my respects to Miz Lilly if you think she's up to havin' company. Baby Heart and I would like to tell her the good news."

His hand feels rough and strange as he slides it over mine. I want to pull away but I don't. I know I have to get use to the touch of a man I have no love or desire for. Might as well start gradual.

Papa Joe clears his throat. "I'll go ahead and tell her y'all want to come in."

John El keeps his promise about not telling Papa Joe our agreement. He's so smooth, I almost forget he knew about Mama Lilly being near death and that he already agreed to pay for everything in exchange for me.

The next day we head to the hospital in Atlanta with Mama Lilly. John El is driving. I'm sitting in front with him. Mama Lilly and Papa Joe are in the back. Mama Lilly is coughing and spitting in a can. Nobody's talking. I take a sideways glance at John El and see a look of disgust on his face. I know he's determined to go through with his promise— for me. He doesn't give a hoot about Mama Lilly.

When he told her we were getting married, a look of horror came into her eyes. She tried to ask me something but went into a fit of coughing and couldn't talk. I stayed out of her room after that. I know if she figures out I'm doing this just so she can get the operation, she will refuse to have it.

I've never been to Atlanta before. Never seen such big, tall buildings. So many cars are zooming around us, I feel a little uneasy. But John El is a good driver. He seems to know where he's going and has no trouble with all the traffic. I relax and ask him, "You ever been up here before?"

"Sure. I have lots of bitniz deals in Atlanta."

We pull up in front of Grady Hospital. It's much larger than it is in my daydreams. I couldn't imagine anything so big. The little one-floor clinic in Marysville with beds in the basement for colored is all I've seen before in the way of a hospital.

When I get inside and see the hugeness of Grady, the nurses walking briskly around in their starched white uniforms and caps, I can't help but shed a tear at all I'm giving up. I like the smell of this place, like medicine and sterilized starched cleanness all rolled together. A place where flies and roaches don't dare come inside. I could have been a part of this bustling city and hospital. I was getting closer to the dream I had since I was a little girl. Today I see it. I can reach out and touch it.

But I will never have it. They think I'm crying for Mama Lilly. But I cry for my lost dream.

We meet with the doctors while Mama Lilly is hustled into an examining room. Tests have to be done. The operation will probably be scheduled for early in the morning. After all of the testing is finished and John El fills out forms committing him to pay the bill, Mama Lilly is wheeled into a private room.

A lady brings a tray with food for her. But Mama Lilly doesn't seem interested in the baked chicken, rice and string beans. Not even the Jello with fruit in it. The sight and smell of food makes the rest of us hungry. We haven't had anything to eat since a little breakfast at seven and now it's three in the afternoon.

John El offers to take us to dinner. Papa Joe doesn't want to leave Mama Lilly. John El and I go in search of food. We discover a big cafeteria right here in the hospital. The food looks good. We take trays and fill our plates with it. We find a corner table and sit down, leaving our plates and drinks on the tray.

I see men and women come in and get trays. I know they're doctors and nurses. The men are wearing white jackets with their names — Dr. so and so —stitched on them. The women have on the white uniforms and white hat with the black band that I admire. They find seats together and talk and laugh like friends while they eat.

Something about them is different. Then I realize what it is. They're colored. All of them are colored. I know we're in a segregated cafeteria. That isn't what's strange. It's all I've ever known. What's strange is all of these colored doctors and nurses. I've never seen more than one colored doctor and one colored nurse in all my fifteen years. What I could've become is right here before me. I break down and sob quietly with my face in my hands.

John El takes my hand and tries to console me. "Baby Heart, stop cryin'. Yo' Mama's gonna be all right."

I snatch my hand away. "It ain't Mama Lilly I'm crying about."

"What you cryin' about then?"

"The colored doctors and nurses. I want to be a nurse. If they can do it and they're colored like me, I know I can too."

His eyes get that hard, mean look. "Stop it! People are lookin' at you. Get them dumb notions out of yo' head. You're gonna be my wife. That oughta be enough for any woman."

We finish eating in silence, pick up some food for Papa Joe and go back to the room. John El says he knows somewhere in Atlanta he can spend the night and leaves. Papa Joe and I settle down in lounge chairs to sleep by Mama Lilly's bedside.

A bad thought hits me like a bolt of lighting: What if Mama Lilly doesn't make it? John El will still have to pay the bill. I will still have to marry him and give up everything I ever wanted. I go down on my knees and pray for God to bring my mother through. I can't bear the thought of giving my life up and losing my mother anyway.

I'm fast asleep in a chair on one side of Mama Lilly's bed and Papa Joe is asleep in his chair on the other side when we're awakened before daylight by a nurse, doctor and orderly who have come to take Mama Lilly. They ask us to get up so they can transfer her to a stretcher and take her to the operating room. Papa Joe is fighting sleep. When he realizes that this is it, he cries out, "Lawd God, please take care of my wife!"

The doctor says, "Calm down. Your wife is going to be just fine. You don't want to upset her."

Papa Joe wipes his eyes with his sleeve. "Can we come with her?"

"No. You can't come in the operating room. But there's a nice comfortable room where you may wait while she's in surgery. Someone will let you know when it's over."

By now they have her strapped to the gurney and wheel her out of the room. She begins to cough. I take Papa Joe's hand and we follow the nurse to the elevator. She ushers us off on the second floor. We follow her around many hallways and twists and turns to the waiting room. It's cheerful. The room is white with chairs covered in soft blue tweed fabric and there are plants on the floor around the walls.

A young lady sits behind a desk dressed in a white uniform with a bright pink pinafore over it. The nurse tells us that she is a candy stripper. I ask, "What is that?" and she says a volunteer who will answer the family's questions and let us know when Mama Lilly is out of surgery.

I'm worried as much as Papa Joe but I'm still fascinated with everything about the hospital. Papa Joe and I sit side-by-side, holding hands. Other colored families are in the room, quietly talking with worried expressions on their faces.

Shortly before noon, John El comes in carrying a bag of sandwiches and bottles of orange soda water. The food smells good. We haven't had anything to eat all day.

"How's Miz Lilly?" he asks as he hands me the bag.

"We don't know. She's been in the operatin' room since early this mornin'" Papa Joe tells him.

"How did you find us?" I ask John El.

"I stopped at the front desk downstairs. They tole me she was in surgery and y'all was in the family waitin' room."

I begin to have a little more respect for John El. He's considerate and I'm impressed that he knows his way around a big city like Atlanta and Grady Hospital. I'm so worried about Mama Lilly that I haven't had much time to think about Bobby Joe.

The candy stripe lady is sniffing our bag of food from where she's sitting in the front of the room. I don't know whether we should eat in this spotlessly clean room so I go over and ask her. She says, 'no' but there's another room right down the hall with tables where we can take our food and eat.

We find the room and open the bag filled with pork chop sandwiches. They're still warm and smell so good we tear into them. John El finds a bottle opener and opens the soda. It's kind of warm. But it's wet and sweet. The food takes our mind off our worries for a little while.

We thank John El for the food and hurry back to the waiting room. The candy striper motions for us as soon as we come through the door. Papa Joe and I look at each other. My heart is fluttering and he looks like he may pass out. We want news, but what if it's bad? What if she didn't make it? We walk slowly to the desk, trying to stall off any bad news.

"Your wife and mother's out of surgery. She's in the recovery room."

I hadn't noticed how pretty the young candy stripe lady is until she said that. Her curly blonde hair looks like cotton candy, her lips like cherries. Maybe it's just the good news that makes her look so pretty.

Papa Joe and I let out a big sigh of relief at the same time and he says, "Thank you Lawd."

I say a silent prayer of gratitude to God. I hug Papa Joe. John El is standing there watching us. I turn and hug him. He seems surprised. I'm surprised, too. I didn't think about it before I hugged him. But I feel like I should be grateful to him. Without his money, Mama Lilly couldn't have had the operation.

Papa Joe asks the candy stripe lady if we can see Mama Lilly. She says we have to wait and talk to the doctor first. He will come to meet with us as soon as he can. We sit back down and wait. We're full and happy that Mama Lilly made it.

We don't have to wait long before the doctor comes. He walks over and introduces himself as Dr. Burton. "We got it all," he says with a big smile as he shakes Papa Joe's hand. "Your wife is stronger than she looks. She came through with flying colors."

Papa Joe thanks him and so do I. "Can we see her now?" I ask.

"She's still sedated. But you all can sit quietly with her if you want to."

Papa Joe and I tiptoe into the room; afraid we might wake her from her rest. She looks pale but peaceful. John El stays in the waiting room.

After about an hour, Mama Lilly opens her eyes and looks at us. "Joe, Baby Heart, when they goin' to do the operation? I want to get it over with before I lose my nerve."

I lean over and kiss her on the cheek. Papa Joe holds her hand. "It's over, Mama. They already operated and you're in the recovery room."

"Why, I just drifted off to sleep."

"No, Ma'am. That was over five hours ago."

"I didn't feel the knife," she whispers. "I saw a angel hooverin' over me just before I drifted off." She talks softly without coughing.

I kiss her goodbye before I leave her alone with Papa Joe. John El is waiting for me.

11

WITH THIS RING

He's sitting patiently looking at a magazine when I return to the waiting room. He stands up, takes my hand and seems genuinely concerned when he asks, "How's she doin'?"

"Good. I think she's gonna be just fine. She's awake now and talking."

"I'm glad. I want to take you on a little shoppin' trip."

"I don't know about that, John El. I don't want to leave her so soon."

"She'll be all right. You jus' said she's fine."

"What you going shopping for?"

"I passed a fine jewelry store not far from here. I want to take you to pick out yo' weddin' rings."

Thump! Thump! My heart is pounding so loud; I think he may hear it. I begin to perspire and wipe my forehead. I don't want a ring. I don't want to marry. I try to stall him. "John El, I haven't brushed my teeth, combed my hair or changed clothes since yesterday. I can't walk into a fine jewelry store looking like this."

"Didn't you bring a change of clothes? You knew we had to spend the night."

I can't lie. He may have noticed the bag in my hand when we left home. "Yeah. I brought something to change in but there's no place where I can wash up and comb my hair."

"Course there is. I'm payin' for a private room for yo' mama. You go on up there and get ready."

I feel like a mouse caught in a trap. "Okay. Wait here."

"Hurry. I think the store closes at six."

I close the door to Mama Lilly's private hospital room, go in the bathroom and wash up, comb my hair and put on my blue sun back dress with a white pique bolero jacket. I leave my hair loose, hanging down below my waist. I admire myself as I look in the mirror and spread on a little lipstick. Then I wonder why I'm getting all pretty for John El. I hate the thought of marrying him. But it's best to move along one step at a time and not think about what I'm doing. I comfort myself with knowing I saved my mama's life.

He's pacing the floor when I get back. "What took you so long?" He looks annoyed with me.

"I had to get ready." I glance at the plants, other people in the room, anything to keep from looking him in the eye. He might see how I'm really feeling, read my thoughts.

He looks me over closely and frowns. "Why you got yo' hair hangin' loose like that?"

"I thought you would like it."

"I do like yo' hair. But I don't want other men lookin' at it. And wipe that lipstick off yo' mouth. There's a gift shop downstairs. I'll stop in there and buy you a kerchief so you can cover up your hair. No wife of mine is gonna run aroun' lookin' like a strumpet."

I open my mouth to say that I'm not his wife yet. Fear closes it before a word escapes. "Can I see Mama Lilly before we go?"

"Make it quick. We need to git there before closin' time."

Inside the recovery room, Papa Joe is nodding. I walk over to the bed with the rails up and look down on my mother. She's sleeping. "Papa Joe, John El wants me to go with him to pick out my rings. You think she'll be okay while I'm gone?"

He arouses quickly from his half sleep and says, "Sho, Baby Heart. Y'all go right along. She's just restin'."

The jewelry store is in the heart of downtown Atlanta. It's big with gleaming counters. Expensive jewelry is locked behind glass showcases. John El swaggers over to a counter with me by the hand. A well dressed white salesman peers at us with curiosity as though we have wandered into the store by mistake.

"How may I help you and your daughter?" the salesman asks.

I cringe at the man's mistake but John El is calm. "First off, this is my fiancée soon to be my wife. I brought her in here to pick out weddin' rings."

The man's face reddens a little. "I have a set you may like." He reaches beneath the counter and places a ring box in front of us that holds an engagement ring and wedding band. The diamond in the engagement ring is so small I'd need a magnifying glass to see it. The gold bands on the rings are very thin. I'm afraid they will break in two if I turn a knob or faucet while I'm wearing them.

John El ignores the rings the man offers us. He looks down at the others on display under the glass, points to a large stone and says, "I had one more like that in mind."

The salesman looks at his watch and clears his throat. "I'm not sure how much you know about diamonds. The one you're pointing to is four carats with astounding clarity. That ring costs a small fortune and we don't finance…"

Now John El's face is turning red. "Did I ask you anything about financin'?" He turns to me and asks, "Baby heart, do you like this ring?"

"I like it fine. But if it costs …"

He cut me off. "Do you like this pear shaped, fo' carat, flawless diamond ring?"

"Sure."

"Let her try it on."

The salesman eyes us suspiciously as he unlocks the enclosure and removes the ring. He's perspiring and seems nervous. I wonder if he's about to call the police. He slides the ring on my finger. It fits loosely.

He holds my hand all the while I have the ring on. Afraid I'm gonna run out the door with it I suppose.

"See, it doesn't fit," he says holding my hand up.

"Most rings don't fit less you get 'em sized," John El drawls.

The man shakes his head and prepares to return the ring to the locked showcase. "I can't have this ring sized unless you pay for it first."

"How much?"

The man gives him a figure so high that I'm sure John El will walk away in disgust. Instead, he reaches in his pocket and comes out with a wad of bills big enough to choke a gorilla. He counts out the money while the man stands with his mouth hanging open.

"Measure her finger and take **my** rings back there so they can make them the right size. We'll wait."

"Yes, Sir." The man hustles off probably thinking more about the color of the money he just made than about the color of our skin.

I laugh. "John El, he just said 'Yes, Sir' to you. I've never heard a white man say that to a colored man before."

"Money buys respect, Baby Heart. You gonna hear a lotta things you never heard before when you become Miz John El Murphy."

While we wait for the rings, I whisper to him, "What happened to your first wife?"

"Ordinarily, I would say that ain't none of yo' bitniz. But I suppose since we gonna get married, you got a right to know. She left me for another man before we had been married a full year. I swore no woman would ever do that to me again. YOU HEAR ME, Baby Heart. Never

Again!" His voice rises, his green eyes burn with fire and his face turns beet red.

"I'm sorry I asked." I pat his hand.

The man returns, smiling, with the pretty black velvet ring box. "Do you want to wear them, or shall I have it wrapped?" He asks me.

I start to say wrap them and give the box to him. John El interrupts and says, "I'll put the engagement ring on her finger now. Wrap the other one and give it to me."

He slips the pear shaped diamond on my finger. It looks more like a big teardrop to me and feels heavy as a boulder— weighing me down, down, down.

12

MAMA LILLY

We get tangled up in traffic jams on the way back to the hospital, slowing us down. I'm nervous and feeling real low. Thoughts of Bobby Joe flood my mind. What is he gonna say when he sees this big rock on my finger? I'll hide it. I can't let him see it until I explain everything. Matter of fact, I think I'll just hide it in a safe place until my wedding day, that I'm hoping will never come.

John El parks the car and we walk through the front entrance to Grady Hospital. I should be happy because my mother is alive. I owe a big part of that to John El. I force myself to reach over and squeeze his hand.

He looks at me, grins and says, "You like that ring, don't you, Baby Heart?"

"The ring is beautiful, John El. But I'm mostly grateful that you helped save my mother's life."

We stop at the front desk to see if Mama Lilly has been returned to her room. The receptionist checks the patient register. She frowns and asks, "Did you say her name is Lilly Turner?"

"Yes, Ma'am. She's my mother."

She looks at me real sad like and says, "I'll call the nurse on duty in the recovery room to let her know you're coming up. Do you know how to get there?"

"Yes, Ma'am. I was up there when she first came from surgery. Is something wrong?"

"Go on up. The nurse and maybe the doctor will be there to talk with you."

Fear strikes through my heart like a dagger. I tear off running to the elevator. John El is trying to catch up with me. I reach the elevator, hop in and the door closes leaving him outside which is fine by me.

I run down the long corridor leading to the recovery room. Before I get halfway there, I hear this strange noise like the high-pitched wail of a wounded animal. I heard that sound once before when I was a little girl. My friend's brother drowned. I heard her mother make the same sound over her dead child. Mama Lilly said she was keening.

I believe the sound is coming from Papa Joe. Tears stream down my face and a scream escapes my throat. It sounds like it's coming from a far away place — not from me. I run into the room only to be stopped in my tracks by the sight of a white sheet over Mama Lilly's face.

Papa Joe is sitting besides her with his head in his hands, making that keening sound. A nurse grabs me, then shakes me and says, "Stop screaming. Calm down, please. We have other patients in here."

I didn't know I was screaming.

"Papa Joe, what happened?" I start to pull the sheet back from her face. The nurse tries to stop me. I push her aside and give her a look intended to frighten the devil himself. I guess she thinks I've lost my mind. I hear her call for help. I pull back the sheet and look at my mother's dead face before they come and hold me back.

"This ring — This damned ring!" I keep screaming the same thing over and over.

"Let me see. What's wrong with your ring, honey?" A man in a white jacket—I don't know if he's a doctor or an orderly— looks at it and shakes his head in surprise. "Why, it's the prettiest ring I've ever seen. Is it too tight?"

"I hate it. I wasn't with my mother when she took her last breath, because I was out with him buying this damned ring. I hate it and I hate him."

"Now, now. You're just in shock from your mother's death. Everything is going to be all right." The nurse says soothingly.

I shake my head. "No, Ma'am. Nothing will ever be right again."

I never felt so close to my mother until she died.

The day of her funeral is one of the hardest in my whole life. All of our neighbors and church members try to ease our grief. But they have no notion of how much I've lost.

Papa Joe is trying to hold himself together with the help of my brothers and sisters. Our family members fill up Rose of Sharon

Church. Many of the other friends and church members stand outside in the sunshine. My brother, Roosevelt, is here from Boston with his wife and five children. All of my sisters and brothers, except Lincoln who isn't married yet, have large families. Being around them eases my pain some.

John El sits with the family even though we aren't married yet. His being beside me is far from comforting. But what can I say? He volunteered to help with funeral expenses so Mama Lilly could be put away nice.

The undertakers come up after we all have viewed the body and paid our last respects. They start to close the casket. Papa Joe and I cry out at the same time "No! Leave it Open."

They move away. I watch my mama and the spray of red and white roses shaped like a bleeding heart all through the funeral.

No family member that I know of has done it before, but when people get up and offer words about how nice my mother was, I decide to say something too. I figure I knew her much better than they did.

I get up and face the people, ready to speak my last words over Mama Lilly. I'm not afraid to speak in public. Everybody says I talk more proper than the rest of the folks in White Chalk. Sometimes I'm teased because of the way I speak. They think I'm putting on airs.

I clear my throat and look out over the crowd through tear filled eyes. All the way in the back of the church I see Bobby Joe standing beside Miz Miller. Our eyes meet and hold. I forget everything I intended to say. I want to run into his arms and stay there forever. I go back to my seat and sit down without saying a word. I hear somebody whisper, "The poor child is overcome with grief."

During the burial ceremony, I have a hard time concentrating.

The preacher is saying, "Ashes to ashes, dust to dust."

I keep craning my neck to see if Bobby Joe is behind me. I don't see him anywhere. I'm nervous and scared. I want him near me. But if he sees John El hanging on to me, my chance to try to explain things may be over. I have to tell Bobby in my own way.

Family and friends gather at my sister Rose's house after the burial to eat and talk. We cling to each other trying to overcome our hurt and put our lives back together without Mama Lilly. It just doesn't seem right leaving her in the cemetery. I kept waiting for Linc or Roosevelt to pick her up out of that casket and bring her back home where she belongs. Those are my childish thoughts. The grown-up, almost married me knows she can never come back home.

John El goes on back to work after the funeral. He mumbles something about coming by later. I'm hoping Bobby Joe and Miz Miller will stop by and I get a chance to talk with him without John El guarding me.

Candy and her mama come in lugging cakes and fried chicken. I run to Candy and whisper in her ear, "I saw Bobby Joe at the funeral. Is he coming over?"

"No. He and Cousin Trudy went back to Marysville right after the funeral. I think Bobby Joe was hurt when he saw John El holding on to you when y'all marched out of the church."

"Oh, My God, Candy. Does he know?"

"Know what?"

"That I'm engaged to John El." I hold up my finger with the ring on it. Candy doesn't seem impressed, just sad.

Candy looks puzzled. "You still going through with it even though Miz Lilly's dead?"

"Yeah. That's the hard part. She's dead, but John El has to pay the hospital bill. They didn't charge him any less because she died. So my debt to him is still the same."

"How you gonna tell Bobby Joe? That boy loves you more than his own life I believe."

"I don't know, Candy. I just don't know how to tell him. But I have to find a way."

13

BACK TO SCHOOL AND BOBBY JOE

John El insists on taking me when it's time to leave for Marysville.
I'm scared to death that Bobby Joe will be over to Miz Miller's when I
come riding up with John El. That's the last thing I want to happen. I
tell him Linc will take Candy and me back but he says,"No, nobody's
takin' my fiancée back but me."

On the way he jabbers on and on about the big wedding we're
gonna have.

"I'm coming over to town Saturday so we can visit Queen Esther
Jones and get her started plannin' the weddin'. We only got a month
and a half to get all the arrangements made," he says.

I turn up my nose and fix my eyes on the trees running by the car
window. "John El, I have to work Saturday," I tell him.

"Work? What you talkin' about, girl?"

"I work at the beauty parlor on Saturdays shampooing for Miz Miller."

"You mean you used to work at the beauty shop. I won't have you hangin' 'round them loose women, fixed up like Jezebels. No tellin' what kind of talk you already heard being 'round them. You coming back with me to White Chalk on Saturdays from now on."

"John El, it's only one month until school lets out for the summer. Can't I keep working till then? I need the money to buy some things for the wedding."

He puffs his chest out. "Anything you want, let me know. I'll pay for it."

"There're some things not proper for the groom to pay for."

"Forgit that proper shit. Yo' folks ain't got no money to pay for nothin'. I knew that when I asked for yo' hand. I pay the cost and I'm the boss. Don't forget it." He slaps the steering wheel. "I don't want to hear another word about no beauty parlor."

I wasn't allowed to invite Candy to ride with us. She had to catch the bus. I feel real bad about that. When I asked if Candy could come with us he didn't lose any time saying, "No." When I asked 'why,' he said, 'I ain't puttin' up with you runnin' with fast girls and loose women. Besides we got bitniz to talk about. Need to be to ourselves.'

He opens the car door for me and carries my things up to Miz Miller's front door. I reach for my belongings, turn to him and say goodbye.

He looks at me, and then swiftly shifts his eyes to the closed door. "Ain't you gonna invite me in?"

"John El, I got home work to catch up on. No time for company."

He gives me his mean squinty-eyed look; "Don't play me for no fool, girl. I know Trudy Miller is that boy's aunt. If I hear you're taking up time with him that'll be the end of school. Don't think I don't have eyes and ears over here in Marysville. I bet he's sitting up in there right now."

I'm shaking and silently praying to God for all I'm worth that Bobby Joe isn't inside. I don't feel his presence. So I gamble and say, "Come on in and look around. Suit yourself. But I don't have time to do no courting tonight."

He says goodbye and struts back to his car like a red bantam rooster. I go inside and collapse on the sofa. Nobody's home, not even Miz Miller.

I preview my future, like a movie, only it's not on a screen.

Everything will be taken away from me on June 11th, the day we get married. Actually, he's already controlling my life. I want to see Bobby Joe so bad it hurts. But I'm too scared to pick up the phone and call him. What if John El doubles back and finds us together. I can't risk getting Bobby in trouble.

From this day forward John El controls my life. Or was it the day he put the ring on my finger? I look at the ring and want to vomit. I go in my room, take it off and hide it under my clothes in the dresser drawer.

I'm so excited about seeing Bobby Joe next day, I can't sleep. I'm up at the crack of dawn, bathing, getting dressed and combing my hair. I'm careful not to wake up Miz Miller. Monday is her day off and she likes to sleep late. My moving around wakes up Candy who sleeps in the other bed in the same room with me. She follows me into the kitchen wearing pink hair rollers and a pink bathrobe. While I make oatmeal for our breakfast, she sits at the table half sleep.

Finally, Candy says to me, "Girl, you were restless all night. Woke me up too early. What's your problem, as if I don't know?"

"Yeah, you know part of it. Maybe you can help me come up with a solution. Got any ideas?"

She yawns and wipes sleep from her eyes with one hand. "What's the part I don't know?"

"John El forbids me to be around Bobby Joe. Says he got spies over here who will tell him if I so much as speak to Bobby. If I do he says he will hurt us both and make me quit school before it lets out for summer."

"You can't help but see him small as Marysville High is."

"I want to do more than see him or talk to him. I've got to feel his sweet lips on mine again. Got to feel the muscles in his arms tight around my waist pulling me close. Feel his hardness against me until I cream."

Candy gives me a mischievous smile, "Why don't you go all the way while you're daydreaming? Nobody will have to know except the two of you."

"John El will know. He'll kill me for sure if I'm not a virgin on my wedding night."

Candy scoops up a spoonful of mushy oatmeal, pauses halfway to her mouth and says, "I think he's just a bully. I bet he wouldn't really kill anybody."

I raise one eyebrow, and say, "You want Bobby and me to test him?" I lean over closer to Candy and whisper across the table, "People say he killed his first wife."

She shrugs her shoulders. "I heard that too. But I also heard she ran away with another man."

"Has anybody ever seen her since?"

"I don't know. Maybe her folks seen her and just don't mention it because they're scared."

"Believe what you want. But I have a feeling he killed her. When I asked him what happened, he said she ran away with another man. His face was twisted with rage, red as a beet and I think if he could, he would have killed her again."

Candy shudders, gets up from the table and says, "I gotta get ready for school."

I get to school way ahead of everybody else. I go into my classroom, sit down and review my lessons. I can't summon the courage to see him just yet. I need time.

When recess comes, I stay at my desk and eat the lunch I brought with me.

Candy begs me to go outside. "Ain't no spies around here, Baby Heart. Bobby Joe is out there waiting to talk with you. Come on."

I shake my head and stay inside.

The shrill ring of the last bell ending the school day sounds. I wonder if he'll be waiting outside for me. I don't have to wonder long. I look up and see him coming through my classroom door, elbowing kids out of his way like he's running a play on the football field. He grabs me by my shoulders, looks deep into my eyes and without a word, he kisses me right there in the classroom.

I take his hand and we move together outside, off the school grounds not noticing anything or anybody around us. I know where he's leading me. We have our secret hideaway where we go sometimes to be alone.

We cross the shallow creek by a foot log, surefooted and steady, without even noticing the water flowing quietly underneath. We've crossed it so many times we could do it blindfolded. On the other side, wild flowers grow near a circle of bushes. We run to the crepe myrtle tree. Its deep pink blossoms are the color of ripe watermelon. We embrace, kiss and slowly sink to the soft ground in each other's arms.

"What's the matter, Baby Heart?" Bobby Joe asks.

I turn my head and look across at the slow moving creek. "What do you mean?"

"You know what I mean. You've been avoiding me all day, like you didn't want to see me after we've been apart over two weeks."

I continue to stare into the distance, wondering how I'm going to tell the boy I love that I belong to someone else, that I can't be seen with him anymore. Tears begin to flow.

He puts his hand under my chin and gently turns my face to his. "Baby Heart, I saw him holding on to you at the funeral. If you want John El, just tell me. I'll understand. I won't bother you anymore."

"Bobby Joe, I'll never want no boy, or man in this world like I want you. But I'm promised to him. I belong to him now."

"Baby Heart, this is America. You're free. Your daddy, John El or nobody else can make you be with someone you don't want."

"You don't understand, Bobby Joe. My daddy didn't make me do it. He thinks I love John El."

"Then why in the world are you doing it? Is it his money?"

"You should know me better than that. I did it to save my mama's life. She needed the operation. We didn't have any way to pay for an operation or doctors and a hospital. John El did. So I made a bargain. I promised to marry him if he paid for the operation. He paid for it and the funeral. My family knows nothing about my bargain. You're the only one beside me and John El who knows why I'm marrying him."

Bobby Joe studies the ground, picks up a twig, and puts it between his teeth and chews on it. Finally he says, "There's gotta be some way out of this. Your Mama is dead. We can run away together. I have folks up North. We can go to Detroit. I'll quit school and get a job in one of the automobile factories. We can get married."

I shake my head sadly, "I won't have you dropping out of school on my account. Anyhow, I can't do that. I got family in White Chalk, Papa Joe, brothers and sisters, nieces and nephews. He already told me, if I run out on him, he'd get even through my folks.

"I'm sorry, but I made a deal. I have to keep my end of the bargain." I look him straight in the eyes through a veil of tears and ask, "Bobby Joe, do you love your mother?"

He studies the ground before he answers softly, "Yes I do. I understand. If I had been in your place and had a chance to save my mother's life, I would have done whatever it took. You're very brave, Baby Heart. I'll always love you. I don't want to cause you trouble so I won't come around anymore."

I clutch my chest. It's bursting with pain as I watch the boy I love turn his back and walk away.

As I sit alone under the crepe myrtle tree I think about what I've lost: my mother, Bobby Joe, my dream of becoming a nurse. All gone. I watch the creek. It ebbs and flows slowly, gently. I think about wading out to where it's deep enough to roll over me, to free me from John El. If I lie down in the deep water and close my eyes, I can fly away.

I sit there thinking about it until the sun turns to reddish gold flames, spreads out on the western sky then disappears over the horizon. I dry the tears from my eyes, get up and walk slowly down the road toward Miz Miller's house.

The sun will rise again in the morning and so will I.

14

MAY 1947

THE WEDDING PLANNER

John El comes early Saturday morning to take me for an appointment with Queen Esther Jones, the wedding planner. He's eager for me to pick dress patterns so Queen Esther can get busy sewing on the wedding gown and bride's maid's dresses. I keep telling him I don't want a big wedding, but he insists.

"I didn't have a fancy wedding when I married Ruby Pearl. Maybe that's why it didn't work out," he says with a frown. "Anyway I want us to do everything in style so folks will know John El Murphy don't spare no costs on his bride. I'm gonna invite guests from Marysville and Atlanta. Of course all the people in White Chalk will be there too."

"And where we gonna put all those folks? You know the church in White Chalk's not big enough to hold more than fifty people." I sound upset and I am— about the whole idea of planning a wedding with him.

John El laughs and says, "I'm thinking about having the wedding on my lawn. I guess we got enough space for everybody from Marysville, White Chalk and half of Atlanta out there."

I look straight ahead through the windshield and don't say anything else. The only wedding I'll ever get excited about is to Bobby Joe. I lean my head back on the car seat, close my eyes and imagine a couple on top of a wedding cake. I'm the bride with my hair hanging down my back. A formfitting white wedding dress, low in front, makes a sharp contrast to my brown skin. It clings to my body like it's molded on while a long white train hangs down the back and billows around the icing on the cake.

Bobby Joe stands besides me in a black tuxedo filled out perfectly by his broad shoulders. The rich reddish brown of his face matches mine. We both wear a happy smile— two chocolate dolls on top of a white wedding cake.

I'm putting the finishing touches on my imaginary bride and groom when John El interrupts my daydreams. "Baby Heart! What's the matter with you? You sleep? We're here at Queen Esther's. Come on get out of the car."

I don't know how long he's been standing there holding the door open. I climb miserably out of the car. I miss not being at the beauty parlor today listening to the idle chatter of the ladies in the shop; hearing all of the gossip like who's having a new baby, and whose husband is messing around with other women. I especially miss the tips that I get when I finish shampooing hair.

They like the way my strong fingers massage their scalps and so the ladies hand me a dime, sometimes a quarter. The doctor's wife gave me a whole dollar bill once. But the undertaker's wife is stingy. She never gives up anything. Anyway, all of that's over with and I'm walking up the steps of the neat white bungalow to the house of the wedding planner.

The front yard is covered with beds of begonias, pansies and impatiens in colors of pink, purple and red. John El rings the doorbell and Queen Esther pops out the door like a Jack-in-the-box. I believe she was standing behind it all the time just waiting for the bell to ring. She's tall and thin, dressed in a flowered print cotton dress and ballerina slippers. The colors of the flowers in her dress match the ones in her yard, pink, purple and red. She makes a low bow, like a curtsy before she invites us in.

"Come into my humble abode Mr. Murphy. It's such an honor to have you and your fiancée choose me to plan your wedding," she says. She beckons us to follow her to a room that's filled with books of dress patterns, flower arrangements, and selections for having invitations printed.

My head is spinning. I feel like running right back out the door.

John El looks around the room at the wedding gowns on fitting forms and flower arrangements waiting to be picked up. There are piles of books we need to go through to pick patterns, invitations and flower arrangements. John El checks his watch, probably thinking about how much time he'll have to miss from the store. Saturday is his busiest day. He doesn't seem too sure of himself anymore. I'm hoping he'll change his mind and say let's forget about a big wedding. Instead he says, "Well, I've been tole that you're the only one doin' this line of work in Marysville."

Queen Esther responds to his statement, "I am the only colored wedding planner who can take care of all of your wedding needs and do it correctly. I make the dresses for the bride and her entire wedding party. My son, Dezi, grows the flowers in our greenhouse. My daughter bakes and decorates the cakes and my other son plays piano and sings."

John El nods. "Looks like y'all got everything covered under one roof. I like that. We won't have to go runnin' aroun' frum place to place."

Queen Esther gives him a gracious smile, then motions for us to sit in two chairs side by side. She sits across from us. "That's not all. My husband is an ordained minister. If you don't have your own, he can perform the marriage ceremony. And my son-in-law is a photographer. The only thing we send out is the printing of the invitations. My neighbor owns the print shop. He's very reliable. Now tell me, have you set the date?"

"June 11th," John El says without hesitation.

Queen Esther fingers the strand of pearls around her neck and looks stunned. "My, my, that leaves just a little over a month. Unless you want something small, I'm afraid that will not give me sufficient time. June is a big month for weddings. I have several orders ahead of you."

I sigh with relief, hoping this will buy me an extra month or two. "That's quite all right Miz Queen Esther. I rather prefer an autumn wedding," I say, striving to match her proper, airish manner of speech.

John El looks at me like I've lost my mind and says, "No Ma'am, that won't do. June 11th is the day I picked and that's when it will be. No costs spared. Whatever you want to add for a rush order, I'm willin' to pay."

Queen Esther primps her mouth and says "In that case, I suggest you pick the invitation first so I can get it to the printer Monday. Next, the bride should pick her gown and the dresses for her wedding party. I have to purchase the material right away and draw up a schedule for fittings."

"You hear that Baby Heart. I told you we should've got started on this earlier. Who you havin' for the maid of honor, bridesmaids, flower girls and ring bearer?"

"Oh my God." I blurt out "I haven't thought about any of that. Why can't we just go to the courthouse like the other folks in White Chalk do when they get married?"

"We're not like the other folks, Baby Heart. Don't worry about it. You got enough kinfolks to do it all."

"Okay. I'll ask Irene to be the matron of honor and Candy can be the bridesmaid."

"Maybe you better ask your sister, Rose. I don't want Irene spoilin' my weddin' walkin' down the aisle knocked up and with a black eye."

I flinch. Even though it's true, I don't want him talking about Irene. She's my favorite sister.

Queen Esther intervenes. She steers us to a long table and hands each of us a book to choose invitations from. "May I bring you a cup of tea while you make your selection," she asks.

"Yes Ma'am, thank you," I say politely.

"A drink of liquor would be more to my likin'," John El says and winks at her.

"I'm sorry. We don't have strong drinks. My husband is a minister." She walks quickly out of the room but returns within a few minutes with my tea, steaming hot in a dainty little china cup, sugar and cream in a matching set and a slice of lemon on the side all sitting on a beautiful silver tray.

I'm beginning to like this woman. I've never seen such classy ways before. I know her from the beauty parlor. Some of the other women laugh behind her back, saying she's a phony who puts on airs and is trying to imitate white folks. But I think maybe I'll be like her. Learn to talk real proper and serve tea in fancy cups.

I don't pay the invitations much attention and let John El pick whatever he likes but when it comes to my wedding dress, I decide to do the picking. Every pattern I like, John El says looks vulgar. We look through about ten books without agreeing. Queen Esther says if we tell her what we want she can design it.

John El loses no time telling her what he wants. She sketches out what he describes. It looks like the dress Bo Peep wears. A pinafore tied in back over a high-necked long sleeved dress with puff sleeves. A headdress that will cover all of my hair and a long white train will set off this outlandish outfit.

I cry out, "No. That's nothing like what I had in mind. It looks like it's for a little girl."

Queen Esther looks at me with pity and says softly, "Mr. Murphy, it is a bit childish for a wedding dress."

John El squints, stands up and puffs out his chest. "That's exactly what I want. That's the one she'll wear."

I cry all the way back to Miz Miller's house. When he lets me out the car, he looks at me and says, "Get used to it, Baby Heart. I'm the man. I make the decisions. I pay the cost to be the boss."

"But why that dress? It looks like something a little girl would wear, not a bride."

"You are a little girl, my little girl. Don't ever go gettin' womanish on me."

He gets back into his car and takes off. I run into the house and collapse on the bed, crying.

There's less than a month left in the school year. I try not to see Bobby Joe. Sometimes we pass each other in the hall when we're changing classes. I find something to study on the wall or the floor to keep from looking at him.

I dive into my lessons and books like they are a balm to heal my wounded heart and soul. I stay inside at recess talking to my teachers or reading. I go to the school library and sign out a lot of books. They're old and well worn, having been sent over second hand from the white school. I read novels, losing myself in the happiness and sorrows of others. I discover Shakespeare. I like Romeo and Juliet. But it's sad. The story is kind of like Bobby Joe and me.

My English teacher is surprised that I'm reading classical literature when I don't have to yet. She's even more astonished that I understand what I'm reading. I don't know why. Reading Shakespeare isn't much different than reading the Bible. I've been reading the Bible to Mama Lilly and Papa Joe since I was a little girl. Papa Joe would say to me, "Baby Heart read us a passage out of the Good Book. Mama Lilly and I can't see well enough to read no more."

I didn't let on that I knew they never learned to read.

And so I spend my last month in Marysville reading and going to fittings for my wedding gown; avoiding Bobby Joe because I can't go through the pain of saying goodbye to him again. When we let each other go under that crepe myrtle tree, it felt like my heart was being ripped from my body. The pain was so sharp it cut like a knife.

The hurt look in his eyes lets me know he's feeling the same thing. We pass in the hallways blindly; acting like we don't see each other, don't know what both of us want is close enough to touch. But if I have to say goodbye to him again, the rolling water in that creek may become my home.

Best to spend my spare time reading and visiting Queen Esther, the wedding planner.

JUNE 11, 1947

MY WEDDING DAY

I didn't sleep at all last night. I lay awake praying that tomorrow would never come. I heard the bedsprings squeak every time Papa Joe turned over in his room. I listened to him snore, heard all the night sounds outside — the Whip – Poor- Wills and the Bob Whites made their birdcalls back and forth to each other through the night. Crickets chirped as they rubbed their legs together. The dogs were silent, probably sleeping. Every creature on earth seemed to be at peace except me.

Light creeps through my window signaling daybreak —my wedding day. I hide my head under the cover to blot it out —try to make it go away.

It's eleven in the morning when Queen Esther arrives at my house carrying my Little Bo Peep wedding dress in a cleaner's bag. Red eyed from crying and no sleep, I shuffle to the door in my old shaggy bedroom slippers and faded duster. She's dressed in a bright blue silk dress that billows out from her tiny waist. Her matching blue pumps are a shiny satin. I wonder vaguely how she plans to keep the red mud from ruining them at the outdoor wedding.

"Good morning, Jolee," she says, beaming with good cheer.

"Good morning Miz Queen Esther," I mutter, with my head down. She looks totally out of place in the country at my unpainted rundown shack.

"I thought you would be almost ready by now. Your wedding starts at one, dear. You better get a move on." She looks me over closely and asks, "Are you okay? You don't look well."

"No Ma'am. I couldn't sleep last night."

"Wedding jitters. A lot of brides get them right before the wedding. It will be all right, dear."

I shake my head and say, "No, Ma'am. I don't think anything will ever be right after today."

Queen Esther purses her lips and looks at me thoughtfully before she speaks. "Well, if you feel that way, maybe you shouldn't go through with it. It's better to call the wedding off than marry with regret. Although I know it would be hard with people gathering from all over. My phone has been ringing off the hook and my mailbox has been full for weeks with RSVPs, all saying yes. A lot of people want to see Mr. John El Murphy take his young bride."

I frown as I think of all the people waiting for the bride, John El waiting for me at the altar in his tuxedo and I never come. Instead

I'm running down the road to the bus stop to go to Bobby Joe in Marysville.

Queen Esther breaks through my thoughts, "What's the problem, honey? Is it because he's much older than you?"

"That's part of it."

"My husband is quite a bit older than I am. It won't matter after you're married."

Queen Esther stands there looking so cool and self-assured. I ask her, "How much older is your husband than you?"

"Eight years," comes her quick reply.

"John El Murphy is twenty-one years older than me. He's thirty-six years old. I'm only fifteen," I say choking back tears.

"Yes. But he has so much to offer you. I'm sure you've seen his house. I had no idea how big and beautiful it is until I went out there to decorate for the wedding. You're going to be a rich young lady, Jolee. A whole lot of women would like to be in your shoes."

"I've never seen his house. I've heard it's big. But I'd rather live out in the woods, eat wild berries and drink rainwater than be cut off from folks I love. I think marrying him makes me poor because I'm losing more than I can tell you. I would gladly trade places with any one of those ladies who want him if I could."

Queen Esther raises her left arm and looks at her watch. "Seriously, you'd better run along and start getting ready. Where should I hang your wedding gown?"

"Just lay it across the bed in this room." I motion to my open bedroom door, made of rough splintery wood, and go outside to bring in the washtub for my bath.

Queen Esther sits in our one good rocking chair on the front porch, fanning while I bathe. When I finish and have on my underclothes, I call her and she helps me into the long white dress and pinafore, and then the headdress goes over my pinned up hair. I put on a little make-up— face powder and pale pink lipstick. I know John El won't like bright red lipstick or rouge. Queen Esther suggests we wait and attach the train when we get to his house so I don't get it wrinkled. I feel foolish and frightened but mostly like a lamb going silently to be slaughtered.

Papa Joe is moving around in his room getting ready. He comes out all gussied up in the new suit Lincoln bought him. His long braids are wound into a bun and pinned at the nape of his neck with a Gertie Perchie hairpin. I've never seen him looking quite so handsome before. He straightens up his broad shoulders and smiles — the first time I've seen him look happy since Mama Lilly died. I don't want to ruin it for him. So I force a smile.

"Baby Heart, what kinda getup is that you got on?" he asks.

"It's my wedding dress, Papa Joe."

"Did you pick it out?"

"No, Sir. John El did all the picking."

Papa Joe throws his head back and lets out a hearty laugh. "It looks like somethin' John El would pick. But you look pretty anyhow." He comes over and gives me a hug. And then we get in Queen Esther's car and head over to John El's for the wedding.

Papa Joe, as well as a lot of John El's other sharecroppers, has been to his home to work on the grounds. But none of them that I know of, including Papa Joe, has ever been inside. I hear he has a lady named

Rosie Petunia who keeps his house clean and his meals on time. I suppose that will be my new job now.

Queen Esther turns onto a dirt road I don't recall going down before. Then we climb a steep hill and soon I'm looking out over one of the prettiest sights I've ever seen — rolling green meadows and cattle standing still as statues in a green pasture look like they are part of a beautiful painting.

The blue sky is streaked with white, setting off this pretty as a picture scene. I thought everything in White Chalk was full of red clay, covered over with layers of white chalk; but not up here, high on a hill far away from poor folks. The air is clearer and everything is green.

My eyes open wide when we approach the house and I see all the white tents trimmed with purple and lavender ribbons. An arbor decorated with purple pansies, small lavender orchids, green foliage and baby's breath stands in the middle of the lawn between the tents. Queen Esther stops the car for me to get a good look. "Jolee, that's where you will say your vows, under that arbor."

I look at the people— more than I can count, walking around on the green lawn. Some are sitting in chairs underneath the tents. They're all dressed in their finest Sunday clothes. Even the poor women from my church are dressed in brightly colored silk and satin dresses. The men are wearing suits and ties.

Voices rise and fall as they make happy conversation. I know some of them have never been in such a beautiful place. They will, no doubt, tell stories to their unborn grandchildren about the day they witnessed John El Murphy and Baby Heart Turner marry in the prettiest wedding they'd ever seen. They'll talk about how special they felt being here.

Sadness overcomes me as I take in this beautiful scene. It's looks like something in a fairy tale. The view is breathtaking but the wrong man will stand underneath that lovely arbor with me. I will repeat vows that amount to a life sentence. I feel no joy, only fear and doom. I begin to perspire and shake.

"Now, now. Calm down, Jolee," Queen Esther whispers as she reaches over and pats my white-gloved hands. "We'll go inside first and attach your train."

I take a hard look at the house for the first time — the house that will become my home or jail for the rest of my life. It's big, really large and so white I wonder if the paint is dry. A covered veranda circles the house meeting at the opening for the steps. When we walk inside I'm truly surprised. There's a small parlor off to the right from the front door. It's furnished with velvet chairs and rich looking side tables. A pretty fireplace in the room has a mantle carved with moons and stars. The room is prettier than anything I've ever seen.

Queen Esther steers me past this room as we continue down the hallway where I see the biggest room I've ever seen in any house. She says it's the ballroom. The guests will be allowed inside after dinner where they will shake our hands in a receiving line. And maybe dance. A trio of musicians is already playing music on the lawn. The ballroom floor is polished to a high shine. Beautiful chairs, I think they're antiques, circle the floor in colors of peach and pale green with small tables between them. I can't imagine John El in this room, let alone me and the other country folks outside. I suppose this house was part of his inheritance and it came to him this way.

We climb a winding staircase and Queen Esther points to the first bedroom we come to. "This is a guest bedroom. We'll put on your train in here and you can check your makeup before you go out to march down the aisle. How do you like your new house so far?"

I shrug. "It's all right. Kind of reminds me of a museum my teacher took us to see on a field trip."

Papa Joe is waiting on the veranda to walk me down the aisle. I don't need to worry about mud or red dust getting on our shoes. The lawn, where we walk to the arbor is covered with white burlap and rose petals are scattered by the flower girls who giggle as they march ahead of me in their pretty lavender, voile dresses and white patent leather shoes, each holding a flower basket. The air is filled with the sweet scent of lilacs that surround the wedding site.

John El stands at the altar looking as uncomfortable as a penguin in the heat, dressed in his black tuxedo and white dress shirt with the black bowtie cutting into his red neck. Papa Joe and I march up and stand facing him.

"Dearly beloved, we are gathered here today to join this man and woman in Holy Matrimony. Who gives this woman to be married?" the preacher booms as though he doesn't know.

Papa Joe says softly, "I do." He waits a few seconds before he releases my arm to John El and takes a seat in the front row. I look over at Papa Joe and see a tear slip slowly down his cheek.

I hold on to John El's arm as the preacher begins the vows.

"Do you, John El Murphy, take this woman, Jolee Turner, to be your lawfully wedded wife to have and to hold, in sickness and in health, for better or worse? If so say, I do."

John El says, "I do" real loud.

The preacher continues, "Will you honor her, cherish her and forsake all others from this day forward, until death do you part?"

"I already honor and cherish her." John El says looking at me with a sly grin.

"Just answer, I do, Mr. Murphy."

" 'Deed I do," he says. John El acts like he's been swigging from his flask or drinking too much of the spiked punch.

The preacher turns to me, "Do you, Jolee Turner, take this man, John El Murphy, to be your lawfully wedded husband? To honor and obey, forsaking all others as long as you both shall live?"

I don't answer. The preacher repeats the question and I mumble real low, "I guess I have too."

The preacher says, "I didn't understand your reply. Please say, I do or I will."

I clear my throat and answer, "I will." All the while I'm scanning the distance hoping I'll see Bobby Joe galloping up the hill, on a white horse or maybe driving his brother's car, coming to carry me away.

The preacher asks, "Is there anyone here who knows any reason why this man and woman should not be joined in wedlock? If so, speak now or forever hereafter hold your peace." He pauses as if waiting for someone to speak.

Bobby Joe is nowhere in sight. Candy is in the front row. I search her face. Maybe she'll raise her hand to speak. She knows why. But she sits perfectly still, smiling. I feel a cold white fog closing around me as I slide slowly to the ground.

When I open my eyes, Queen Esther and Mother Adams from Rose of Sharon Baptist Church are on their knees. Mother Adams is cradling my head while Queen Esther holds a vial to my nose. The strong unpleasant odor of smelling salts brings me back to the wedding scene. I try to focus. John El is bending over me looking worried. They lift me up.

"It's all right, you just fainted," Queen Esther whispers. "It happens to more brides than you realize. Some grooms too."

My knees wobble. I stand holding on tight to John El's arm, hoping not to embarrass myself more than I already have.

The preacher smiles and says, "I now pronounce you man and wife. Mr. Murphy, you may salute your bride."

John El raises his hand and salutes me like a soldier. The minister and the crowd burst out laughing.

"I mean you may kiss your bride," the minister says.

John El raises my veil, squints at me with disapproval before he gives me a quick peck on the cheek and lowers the veil again.

"You're supposed to turn it back off her face, John El so we can all see the bride," someone yells out.

"Not until you wash that war paint off yo' face. Nobody is gonna look at my wife made up like a Jezzy Belle. Go inside and wash it off." He hisses at me.

I turn and run, watering my wedding bouquet with my tears. I barely notice the long tables loaded with food and the two chefs standing erect with tall white hats on their heads behind the tables. Through a haze of tears, I see a barbequed pig with an apple in its mouth in the center of the table. I begin to bawl out loud for the pig whose life was taken for this sorry affair.

My maid of honor and bridesmaids catch up to me and support me into the house. I collapse onto the bed in the guest bedroom, crying my eyes out. They try to comfort me but I refuse to be consoled. I want to feel the pain that is tearing through every nerve in my body. Feeling it is better than being numb. When it hurts, I know I'm still alive. If

I'm alive I can fight— find some way out of this mess. I tell them, "Go away. I want to be alone."

John El comes up looking for me when I don't come back. He asks, "What's wrong with you?" He sounds peeved. "Our guests are waitin' downstairs to greet us in the receivin' line."

"I don't feel good," I mumble, turning over to look at him.

His face is red with anger. "Ain't nothin' wrong with you. You're just poutin'. Get up from there and come on down stairs before I get a strap to yo' behind."

"My daddy never whipped me. You sure in hell better not try it," I yell at him.

He snatches me up by one arm, drags me to the bathroom where he takes a washcloth and washes the makeup and tearstains from my face. Then he says, "I ain't yo' daddy, I'm yo' husban'. You goin' downstairs with me or you gonna let everbody hear Miz John El Murphy get her first whippin'?"

Meek as a lamb, I follow him downstairs.

Beautifully arranged roses perfume the ballroom with their fragrance. I inhale the sweet air and stand shaking hands in the receiving line with a smile pasted on my face and tears in my heart. I don't want to cause trouble. I know if Linc and Papa Joe hear him beating me on my wedding day, somebody will go to hell this evening.

16

MY WEDDING NIGHT

After all the guests leave I don't know what to do with myself. I sure don't want to be alone with John El Murphy. I know what happens on the wedding night. I go upstairs and look through the bag of clothes I brought with me, trying to find something to change into so I can go downstairs and help Miss Rosie Petunia and a bunch of other ladies who are cleaning up dishes and putting away food. I want to save some of that food for Irene and her scrawny kids.

John El walks up behind me, puts his hands on my breasts and squeezes real hard. Wincing from pain and anger, I push his hands off me.

"What you think you doin', little girl? You're my wife. All of this is mine now. You can't refuse yo' husband." He feels my breasts and my butt. "You're in the wrong room. Come along with me."

He takes my hand and leads me down the hall to a different room. This bedroom is bigger. The spread and matching draperies have a white background with green-stemmed pink roses. Two large chairs sit in the corners of the room, one green and the other pink. Both are velvet. Pretty little lamps are on the tables on each side of the bed. I look at the room in wonder. "Is this my bedroom?" I ask him.

"This is **our** bedroom." He opens a dresser drawer, pulls something out and lays it on the bed. "Put this on."

I look at the skimpy red nylon outfit that is see- through sheer and ask, "What is that?"

"Baby doll pajamas for my Baby Heart."

"My sister Rose gave me a gown to wear tonight," I say as I search through my bag of belongings, thinking about the long pink gown that will cover my body.

"Forget it," he says, reaching for me. "I want you to wear this. I been dreamin' about you in these red baby doll pajamas."

"They don't look like pajamas to me. These little things won't cover up a mouse."

"That's the idea. You're not supposed to cover up with me. Now put these on. Turn that long pretty hair loose and come on to bed. I got somethin' else for you."

Clutching the baby doll pajamas to my chest, I turn to walk out of the room. He calls me back. "Where you think you goin'?"

"To change my clothes."

"Change them right here where I can watch you. I'm glad you're modest, but I'm yo' husban'. You ain't supposed to hide nothin' frum me." He strips down to his boxer shorts and stretches out on the bed.

I feel ashamed taking my clothes off in front of him. I've never let a man see me naked. All those wedding vows haven't changed how I feel about him. What I'm doing doesn't seem right. He's still John El Murphy, the man who thinks he owns us. I have known him all of my life and never liked him. The way he treated me today makes me dislike him even more.

Some words spoken by a minister and a piece of paper haven't changed the way I feel about him at all. I ask him to please put out the lights or turn his head. He won't do either. His unblinking green eyes stay fixed on me like they want to swallow me whole.

Brushing my hair always takes a lot of time. Now I count slowly to one hundred as I stroke it, stalling for time. I'm sitting on a little vanity bench in front of the mirror attached to the dresser, wearing the sheer red baby doll get-up. Suddenly, he springs up, scoops me in his arms and carries me to bed.

His breath reeks of alcohol. He's panting and squeezing me. I lie real still with my legs crossed tight and pray for this night to end. Then he straddles me, takes one of his boney knees and pushes my legs apart. Something hard that feels like a dagger enters me. Pain shoots through my private parts like flickering flames of fire and I cry out. That excites him more. He pumps fast, up and down.

Just before he rolls off me, he takes his finger and brushes the tears from my cheeks. "Don't cry, my little Baby Heart. It only hurt like that because you were a virgin. It won't be so bad the next time. You may even get to like it some. But good wives don't ever like it too much. A woman who enjoys screwin' turns into a whore runnin' from man to man."

"I would never do that to you," I whisper.

"You came to me pure, just like you promised. I appreciate that. You stay true to me and I'm gonna give you anything you want. But don't ever cheat on me. I swear I'll put you in yo' coffin before I let you make a fool out of me with another man!"

I can't see his face but the sound of his voice sends a cold chill up my spine. I know he means what he says.

"John El, can I go to the bathroom now?" I ask quietly.

"Go on. Wash yo'self up. Don't be scared if you see blood. That's because I bust yo' cherry."

I stumble to the pretty bathroom holding the skimpy baby doll pajamas in front of me. The stuff that squirted out of him feels sticky on my thighs. It has a strange sterile odor like the smell in the hospital. I scrub hard trying to remove his scent from my body. I see blood on the bath cloth.

I know all about cherries and virgins. Everybody talks about saving it 'till your wedding night with the man you love. I was saving mine for Bobby Joe. Now it's gone. Not to the man I love but to the man I hate.

17

MIZ JOHN EL MURPHY

At first I can't remember where I am. I look around the strange room and rub the sleep from my eyes. Over in the corner, John El sits on the green velvet chair already dressed in blue jeans and a pale blue denim shirt. He's putting on his socks. I try to sit up but the soreness from his workout on top of me last night causes me to put my head back down on the pillow.

"Good mornin', Baby Heart. How you feelin'?" John El drawls.

"I'm sore and sleepy. I didn't get much sleep because you were snoring. I didn't sleep the night before either. I don't feel so good. But I'll get your breakfast ready quick as I can." I swing my legs out of bed.

"I don't need you to cook for me. Rosie Petunia is downstairs makin' my breakfas'. She'll keep on doin'all the cookin' and the housework."

I look at him and blink, "John El, I'm confused. I thought a big part of being a wife was to take care of my husband and the house."

He's bent over, lacing his heavy work boots as he speaks, "That's because you ain't ever known a colored man who could afford hired help. I bet you know that white men, even ones who don't make much money like the mailman for instance, pay colored women to take care of everything so their wives— Miss Ann we call 'em — can sit on their behinds and look pretty. Well, you my Miss Anne.

"You don't need to worry yo' pretty little head about no cookin' an' cleanin'. I told you I was gonna take good care of you." He sits up straight, smiles and winks at me.

"If you don't want me to work at home, I can run the store. I'm real good at math. I can wait on customers and keep your books straight while you're at the chalk mine."

John El's good mood changes the minute those words leave my mouth. His face reddens and his eyes squint suspiciously. "Are you crazy? You seriously think I'd allow you to work in the store with all kinda men comin' in and out, some of 'em half drunk and usin' cuss words. I don't even want you comin' down there. Tell me what you need or send Rosie Petunia."

"What am I supposed to do all day?" Then I get a bright idea and say, "Maybe I'll go back home and help Papa Joe with his field work."

He comes over and sits next to me on the bed. He takes my hand in his and looks directly at me. He speaks slowly and clearly like he's talking to a child. "Listen to me and listen good. I'm goin' to explain my rules to you just once. If you wanna stay out of trouble, you best remember them. My wife don't work in cotton fields. She don't get her hands dirty cleanin', cookin' and washin' dishes. She don't go runnin' in and out of folks houses. And nobody comes here. She looks pretty just for me. When she has to go out, she keeps her hair covered and her eyes off other men."

Terror strikes in my heart. Is this man going to cut me off from my family, I wonder? I don't want to hear his reply but I say it anyway. "John El, I hope you don't mean I can't see my folks."

He shrugs his shoulders. "You can see 'em on Sundays at church. They can't come here and you can't go to their houses."

The distress I'm feeling comes out in a strained sound thin and sharp as a straight edged razor blade, "I don't see how I'm going to keep that rule. My folks are all I've got. They mean the world to me."

He raises an eyebrow and looks at me with a puzzled expression, "You forgot the vows you took yesterday? You vowed to forsake all others and cleave only to me. You promised to obey me, woman. You goin' back on your weddin' vows already?"

Oh, Lord what have I done? I think. But I answer humbly, "No, John El. I'm not going back on my word. I'll obey you."

"You make sure you do. Rosie Petunia will tell me if you got folks trampin' in and out of here or if you're out runnin' aroun' while I'm gone."

Slowly it sinks in. Now I understand. Rosie Petunia is more than the maid. She's my prison guard.

18

ROSIE PETUNIA & MIZ MURPHY

After he leaves, I drift back off to sleep.

The sound of the grandfather clock striking nine wakes me up again. I hop out of bed, go to the bathroom and run a tub of warm water. All the while I'm soaking, I'm wondering at how John El can get running water and electricity. I didn't think it was possible to have modern conviencies in White Chalk— never seen a country house with indoor plumbing and hot water before. I got used to such things in town at Miz Miller's. But how does he get it hooked up way out here in the country, I wonder.

I walk into the gleaming kitchen. A lingering scent of the country ham that John El had for breakfast is in the air. It whets my appetite.

I notice the electric stove and white Frigidaire and think this house surely belonged to a Miss Anne at one time. Not even Queen Esther or Miz Miller have houses nearly this pretty.

Rosie Petunia is sitting at the kitchen table shelling butter beans. She looks at me with a blank face and asks, "What you want for breakfas', Miz Murphy?"

I look around for Miz Murphy and realize she's talking to me. "Please call me Jolee or Baby Heart, Miz Rosie Petunia. Don't mind me. Just go ahead with what you're doing. I'll fix my own breakfast. I learned how to cook on an electric stove when I lived in town."

She jumps up and squints at me, looking a lot like John El — light skinned, green eyes. She's short and fat. He's rawboned. Her hair is reddish like his but it's kinky. Still they bear a striking resemblance but I keep my thoughts to myself.

"You tryin' to get me in trouble with the boss? I'm the servant. You the boss lady. You call me Rosie Petunia. I call you Miz Murphy. I cook yo' breakfast. You sit down and wait."

"But you look way older than me. Even older than John El. My mama told me to always put a handle on the names of grown folks."

She looks at me impatiently, with her hands on her hips, and asks, "How many servants did yo' mama have?"

"None. But she told me when she worked for a white family once the children called her Mammy or Auntie."

"You ain't no chile and I ain't about to go back to no old timey slavery talk like that. Just call me Rosie Petunia and we'll both stay out of trouble."

She looks peeved. I want to make friends with her. If she's my keeper it won't do to make her mad, I think. So I sit down and keep my mouth shut. When she asks if I want a cup of coffee, I say, "Yes, thank you, Rosie Petunia."

I try to strike up a conversation with her while she's cooking my breakfast. "Miz Rosie ... I mean Rosie Petunia, how does he get running water and electricity way out here?"

"There're springs all over this land. He gets the water pumped from the spring."

"And the electricity? I don't see lines anywhere."

"He uses generators. If you rich enough, you can get anything," she says slowly while she scrambles my eggs.

"I never knew he was rich — I mean really rich like this."

"John El's got so many head of cattle, I doubt if he knows how many with little calves bein' born every day. His corn and cotton fields cover miles and miles of acres. Add the chalk mine and general store to all that, and you didn't think he was rich?" she asks, scorn dripping from each word.

I don't know if the scorn is intended for John El or me. But I keep my mouth shut and go back upstairs after breakfast. I change the linen on the bed, make it up and dust the furniture. Then I go into the other bedrooms — there are four in all. There's a fifth door but it's locked. I think about how comfortable these rooms would be for Irene and her children. I doubt they'll ever see them much less lay their heads on one of these pretty, fluffy pillows.

The clock strikes three and at the same time I hear John El's voice in the kitchen. His boots make a thudding sound on the stairs. He finds me in one of the spare bedrooms.

"How's my little Baby Heart?" he asks putting his arms around my waist.

I tense up tight as the strings on a guitar at his touch, but I don't dare push him away. "I'm okay."

"I see you're checkin' out the extra bedrooms, just like Goldilocks. This one will make a fine nursery for our first baby, don't you think?"

This is another shocker for me, right up there with being called Miz Murphy. I honestly hadn't thought about having babies with John El. My thoughts had all been filled with the fright of marrying him, losing Bobby Joe and trying to figure a way out short of suicide. Now I think with alarm, after what he did to me last night, I could be pregnant already.

"John El, I been meaning to talk to you about that. I think we should wait a year or two before we have babies — give us a chance to get to know each other better before kids start taking up our time."

He pats my stomach. I hope I got a little seed growin' in there right now. I'm thirty-six years old and don't have a chile to my name. I'm goin' to keep you filled up with a baby every year. You better not do anything to stop 'em frum comin', either. Now, come on downstairs and have dinner with me. I have to go to work down at the store after I eat.

His pants are covered with chalk. I know he's been working hard all day but I'm glad he'll soon be gone. I hope he will come back too late and tired to screw me again tonight.

I have to find a way to gain Rosie Petunia's confidence. By washday, which is Wednesday, I see an opportunity. Every day, I have been asking her to let me help with the housework and cooking but she always scowls at me and refuses my offer.

Today she heads off to the washroom with a basket full of clothes and I follow her. The room contains a washing machine with a wringer attached to put the clothes through before hanging them on the line to dry.

I watch her struggle trying to wring sheets out by hand before I ask, "Rosie Petunia, why don't you put them through the wringer?"

"Uh, huh. I'm scared of that thing. The only time I tried to use it my hand got mangled up in there. I thought it was goin' to tear my whole arm apart before I could cut it off. I was black and blue for a month." She shakes her head, looking at the wringer with terror in her eyes.

"Let me help you. I'll feed the sheet in while you hold on to it when it comes out the other end."

She stands back and looks me squarely in the eyes, "Why you want to help me so bad? I think you tryin' to get me fired. You'll run back and tell Mr. Murphy I'm lazy and you have to help get the work done."

"I would never do that. I see how hard you work while I sit with nothing to do. I won't mention it to him."

She throws her hands up in the air, "I can't stop you. But if that thing gobbles you up, don't tell him I asked for your help."

I guide the sheets into the wringer without any problem. I can tell by the look on her face that she's beginning to like me.

The next morning while we eat breakfast together we begin to talk. Mainly we talk about little things like the weather, other people who work around the place taking care of the cattle, chickens and fields.

By the middle of the second week, I think I have her confidence. I ask, "When is your day off, Rosie Petunia?"

"Day off? I don't get no day off."

"You mean to tell me you work from sunup to sundown everyday and never go anywhere?"

"Yes Ma'am."

The 'Yes Ma'am' didn't sound like it was out of respect but more like what is called sarcasm. She gets up from the table with a stack of dirty dishes in her hands.

I feel sorry for Rosie Petunia.

I am allowed to attend church on Sundays where I get to see my folks. John El takes me and comes back for me right after the service. But my folks and I find a way to hug each other and talk. We sit together, just about taking up all the seats on one side of the little church. Being close to them for one day out of the week keeps me going. But Rosie Petunia can't go anywhere.

While she washes the dishes, I dry them. "Rosie Petunia, don't you go to church anywhere?"

"Nope. Don't have time for that."

"Why do you let John El treat you like a slave, Rosie Petunia?"

"He pays me well. Anyhow there's a lot you don't know about John El and me."

I think I'm making a joke but it doesn't go over too big, when I say, "Y'all look a lot alike. Don't tell me he's your son."

Rosie Petunia drops a plate. As it clatters to the floor, breaking into many small pieces and shards, she looks at me with tears in her eyes.

"I'm sorry Miz Rosie Petunia. I was just joking. I didn't been to hurt your feelings." I run to find the broom and dustpan to sweep up the glass.

"Now you stop that," she says sternly. "If he walks in here and catches you cleaning up, I'll have hell to pay." Her face is red and tear-streaked. She takes the broom from me and while she's bending over sweeping the glass onto the dustpan, she says "No he's not my son. But you're close. He's my brother."

I'm shocked. "Why would your own brother treat you like he does? Besides he's never mentioned to me that you're his sister. I know his mama is dead and he told me he didn't have any brothers or sisters."

"He don't consider me his sister. We're half. We had different mamas but the same ole white daddy. When Mr. Scott, I'm sure you know that was his daddy's name, died he left everything to John El. He never so much as left me a good-bye note. But I was his oldest chile. I'm ten years older than John El. My mama came here to work for Mr. Scott when she was a young girl, about yo' age.

"He lived with her like a wife or mistress, whatever you want to call it. Anyhow, they had me. I was born right here in this house and lived here until I was eight years old. Then he met John El's mother, Lizzie. She was fourteen and pretty as a picture when he first noticed her come into the store. He took her in and kicked me and my mama out. We had to go to work in the fields pickin' cotton with the rest of his field hands and live in a shack down the road."

"So why are you doing this? Don't tell me it's out of love for your baby brother."

"First, you tell me why you married him."

"Well, I wanted the security of what he had to offer," I fib. I don't trust her enough to tell her my real reason. Or maybe it's just too painful to say I traded my freedom for my mother's life but she died anyway.

"Promise you won't say a word to him about any of this," Rosie Petunia whispers.

I cross my heart just like I used to do in grade school when Candy would trust me with a secret, "Cross my heart and hope to die if I ever tell," I say.

She clears her throat and searches my face with her eyes trying to see if I'm telling the truth, I suppose. When she seems satisfied, she continues, "Well like I said ole man Scott, my ole white daddy, died and didn't leave a penny to me and all of this to him. John El sent for me about a month after Mr. Scott's death. He says to me, 'Rosie Petunia, the ole man wants me to take care of you if you'll take care of me. He told me you're his first born chile and asked me to share my inheritance with you if you will live here and take care of the house and everything for ten years. As a matter-of-fact, he's got it in the will.'

"It's been eight years. I only got two more to go then I'll be free and own half of everything. How long you got before you get yo' freedom, Miz Murphy?" she asks it like she's mocking me for feeling sorry for her.

"Did you see the will or get anything in writing?" I ask her.

"Don't worry about that. I know how to take care of myself." She gathers up her mop and bucket and waddles off upstairs.

19

MARRIED LIFE

The days drag by with nothing to do but talk to Rosie Petunia and go to church on Sundays. I try being nice to John El, hoping he'll give me more rope. While I'm sitting on his lap one evening, I ask "John El, will you teach me how to drive?"

"Hell, no," he replies as he strokes my hair. John El loves my hair. I think sometimes about cutting it off and giving it to him to play with. Maybe he will leave me alone. He likes for me to sit on his lap in baby doll pajamas and pretend I'm a little girl. Sometimes, he asks me to suck my thumb or a lollipop.

"Why won't you teach me to drive?" I poke my lips out in a pout.

"A woman ain't got no bitniz drivin' a car. Anywhere you need to go, I'll take you. I take you out for a ride on Sundays after church, don't I? We can go into Marysville to the picture show sometimes if you want."

"I would like to go shopping for clothes and things for the house. It would just be a waste of your time to go along."

"I'll be the judge of that," he says and changes the subject.

We've been married for a month, and I haven't seen hide nor hare of my period. By August it's getting near to the second month and I still haven't had my period. I'm scared, real scared. Something is growing in me. I know it for sure when I start getting an upset stomach every time I smell or see food.

I'm pregnant. I don't tell anybody. If I don't breathe word of it out on the air, maybe it will go away. Every time I go to the bathroom I look to see if there's a drop of blood or a little pink on the white toilet paper but there's no sign.

I feel trapped. I can't see Candy or talk with her like I used to. She will soon be going back to Marysville to continue high school. She'll get to talk with other girls and boys, go to ballgames and dances, and most of all she'll get an education while I'm stuck out here in the country with nothing to do and if that's not bad enough, I'm pregnant. I hate my life. I envy Candy and I hate this thing growing in me.

At the end of the second month I know my childhood is over and accept that I'm having a baby. I tell him, "John El, I'm pregnant." My voice is flat and I feel numb from head to toe.

He grins from ear to ear. "Baby Heart, this is what I've hoped for— my own family. You give me a boy and you can have anything you want."

Without hesitation, I say, "I want to learn to drive."

He shakes his head from side to side but says, "I'll teach you after the baby comes."

"I want to learn now. I should go to the doctor. He'll probably want me to come back at least once a month. I need to know how to drive to get there."

"I'll take you to the doctor. You think I want Miz John El Murphy going to the doctor by herself? I'm gonna take good care of my wife and baby."

"John El, please! What if I get sick or go into labor way out here and can't reach you or the doctor."

"I'm gonna see about gettin' a telephone here and at the store. That's all you need—a telephone."

"John El, that big Cadillac is sitting in the yard and yet I can't even drive for help if I have to. I can't take myself to town to shop for supplies or anything. You say I can have anything I want. Well that's what I want, to learn how to drive and be able to go a few places by myself."

"Okay. I'll try to teach you to drive. It's not as easy as you think, though. And even if you do learn, I'm not gonna have you runnin' up and down the road by yo'self. Rosie Petunia will have to go with you."

"That's fine with me," I say with a smile, content that I have won one small victory.

Driving turns out to be easy. I get the feel of the car right away. I hold it on the ruddy clay roads without swaying or running into ditches even when I feel it trying to pull to the side. John El is surprised I catch on so fast. Driving on the paved roads is a breeze for me.

By the end of summer, he takes me into Marysville to get a driver's license and lets me drive around in traffic. I still hold my own. He seems proud that I can drive so well but at the same time I can tell he's scared of losing control.

The day that the phone is installed, I feel another little breath of freedom. Miz Miller has a phone. I can call her and Candy from time to time and maybe I'll even call Queen Esther. John El says the phone is just for emergencies but since I'm Miz John El Murphy and preparing to have a baby, I figure I can make some rules of my own. And one of them is to talk on this telephone when I feel like it. The other is to drive my car when I get a notion.

20

SEPTEMBER 1947

BOBBY JOE

As soon as Candy goes back to school in September, I call her up on the telephone. I'm eager to find out what's going on at Marysville High and especially to hear something about Bobby Joe. I know I shouldn't ask about him much less think about talking to him. But no matter how hard I try, I can't get him off my mind.

After we say our hellos, I blurt it out, "Candy, have you seen Bobby Joe?"

"I saw him once since I've been back. He came by the house to see Miz Miller and me."

"Did he ask about me?"

"Yeah. He says you're all he thinks about. That's why he's not coming back to school. He's going to join the army. Says he can't get used to you not being here. He feels like if he goes away to the service, he may be able to get over you."

"Oh, Candy. He shouldn't drop out of school. He's so smart. If he finishes high school and goes on to college, he could be a football coach like he dreams of. I can't stand the thought that he's dropping out of school because of me. Suppose he gets injured or killed." I start crying.

"Baby Heart, there's no war going on. This is the best time for him to be in the army."

"Somebody may start one, Candy. I heard some talk on the radio about a place called Korea where trouble is brewing. "

"Baby Heart, it's not your fault what Bobby Joe does. He's got to decide what to do with his life just like you had to make a hard choice. I'm sorry I told you."

"Candy, I have to talk to him. Maybe I can get him to change his mind and go back to school."

She hesitates before she says, "I'm pretty sure he already enlisted."

"Oh My God! Candy I've got to talk to him before he leaves. John El goes to work down to the store every evening around four and doesn't get home until after eight. Do you think you can get Bobby to come over to Miz Miller's tomorrow evening? I'll call at five."

"I don't know, Baby Heart. You're a married woman now and your husband is a dangerous man. I would feel bad if I get involved, and he hurts you or Bobby Joe."

"Candy, you're my best friend. You're the only one who can help me. Please do this one thing for me. I won't ask you to do anything else. I have to talk to him one more time before he leaves or I'll lose my mind. John El will never know. If he's home, I won't call."

"What if he comes home while you're on the phone or if somebody on the party line hears you and tells John El?"

"I can hear his truck a mile away. And we have a private line."

"What about that Rosie Petunia woman? She could eavesdrop on the phone and tell him."

"We don't have but one phone. Besides, she wouldn't do that. Rosie Petunia and I are tight."

"Okay. I'll tell Bobby Joe."

I'm excited and floating on air all day anticipating the sound of his sweet voice — wondering what we will say to each other. I'm tingling with life —feeling more alive than I've felt since the last day we were together down by the creek in the shade of the crepe myrtle tree. That was one of the saddest days of my life but every nerve in my body was alive. I have been going through the motions, not feeling anything since the day I gave him up. I'm tired of being numb.

The grandfather clock in the hallway strikes five. At the same time Rosie Petunia heads upstairs to take a nap, look through the Sears and Roebuck Catalog, or whatever she does on her free time between five and seven when she returns to the kitchen to prepare supper. I creep into the front parlor where the new telephone is installed and close the leaded glass door behind me. I can see Rosie Petunia if she returns and from this location I can hear John El's truck if it comes rumbling up the road early.

"Hello," Candy answers on the first ring.

"Candy, is he there?" I'm anxious to hear his voice. I don't even ask Candy how she feels.

"He's right here. Hold on."

"Baby Heart." The sound of his voice makes me weak. I wish I could go through the phone and touch him. I see his face in my mind — his deep rich chocolate skin, his soft brown eyes. I imagine he's smiling. I want to put my finger in the dimple that sinks in on the right side of his face when he smiles.

"Hey, Bobby Joe." I'm overcome. I can't get my breath, can't find words to say more. I guess he feels the same. For a while we say nothing, just listen to each other breathe.

Finally he whispers, "I love you. Always will."

"I love you too. Can't stop thinking about you though I know I shouldn't."

He clears his throat. "We can't help how we feel. That's why I decided to go away. Maybe if I'm far away in the army, the distance will take my mind off you and help ease my pain."

"I want you to stay in school. I can't stand the thought that I'm causing you to lose your dream of becoming a coach."

"I can finish school on the G.I. bill. I'll still reach my goals. It just won't be the same without you."

"Bobby Joe, I have to see you one more time. Can we figure out a way?"

"I don't want to get you in trouble. Your husband might hurt you if he finds out."

"I don't care if he hurts me. I'm already hurting. I have to see you."

"Do you want me to come out there and get you?"

"No. I can drive now. I'll come to town. I have to bring Rosie Petunia with me. I'll leave her over to Miz Miller's."

"Can you find your way to Gray's Crossing?"

"Sure."

"There's a motel for colored there, right off the highway. Pull your car behind the motel. I'll find you."

"What time?" I ask him.

"Whatever time is good for you."

"It would be best for me to come early, right after he leaves for work. I'll get there by eight in the morning. I have to leave no later than one in the afternoon to be back before he comes home for dinner."

"Be careful."

We hang up. I whirl around the room filled with excitement and fear, impatient for tomorrow morning to come.

21

A DAY IN PARADISE

I pretend to be asleep when John El gets up. As soon as his truck pulls out of the yard, I jump up and start getting ready. I call down the stairs to Rosie Petunia, "Get ready. I need you to go to town with me."

She comes to the bottom of the stairs and looks up at me with her hands on her hips. "What you talkin' about Miz Murphy? We ain't had breakfas' yet. Anyhow the stores don't open 'til nine. We got plenty time."

"Rosie Petunia, get ready now! I'll see to you getting breakfast when we get to Marysville." My voice is demanding. I didn't even know I could speak with such authority.

I bathe and put on a yellow sun-back dress with spaghetti straps that I haven't worn since I married. I add the bolero jacket that goes with it and put on flat sandals. I grab a kerchief to tie around my hair and dab perfume behind my ears. Then we're off.

Rosie Petunia is huffing and puffing behind me as I run to the car. "I don't know what in tornation is so important in town that we got to get there before the stores open," she grumbles, clutching her pocket book.

"Did I say anything about going shopping? I've got an early appointment with Doctor Scott. I may be expecting." I'm glad I hadn't mentioned my pregnancy to her before. The doctor's appointment gives me a reasonable excuse to leave her at Miz Miller's.

Rosie Petunia shoots me a quizzical glance. "John El know about this?" she asks.

"No. Don't mention a word to him when we get back. I want to surprise him if it's true."

"I'm gonna starve while I'm sittin' around in the doctor's office all day waitin' for you to be seen. I should've brought along some lunch."

"Rosie, I have a great idea. I can drop you off at my friend Miz Trudy Miller's. She'll fix breakfast for you and I heard she just bought a television set. You can stay there and watch television."

"A tele...what?"

"Miz Miller is one of the first people in Marysville to own one. I haven't seen it myself. But it's a great invention, Rosie Petunia. You know how you like to listen to 'As The World Turns' on the radio? Well, now you can watch it on television kind of like going to the movies."

"You don't say. I ain't been to the movies more than once or twice in my life. Maybe, I'll stay over to her house while you go to the doctor if she don't mind. I hate goin' to Doctor Scott's office anyhow. Knowin' he's my blood uncle, yet he don't own me don't set well with me. But

I don't know why I let that bother me. My own brother don't own me and he's a colored man."

I reach over and pat her puffy hand. "Don't worry, Rosie Petunia. The Lord will work it all out in due time."

We pull up to Miz Miller's house at seven. I rush up to the door, leaving Rosie Petunia who's waddling along behind me. I guess Candy heard my car turn into the driveway. She runs to the door and hugs me. Miz Miller is right behind her. They both are glad to see me.

"This is Rosie Petunia" I introduce Rosie Petunia to Miz Miller who makes her feel right at home.

"I'm pleased to meet you, Rosie Petunia. Come on in. I'm making breakfast for Candy and me. I'll add some more to the skillet if y'all will join us," Miz Miller offers.

"I don't want to be a bother," Rosie Petunia says, rubbing her fat hands together, while she practically drools at the smell of ham cooking.

"You're no bother to me. I'm pleased to have y'all visit." Miz Miller is smiling and sincere.

I get Miz Miller's eye. "I have a doctor's appointment at eight. Is it okay for Rosie Petunia to stay here? She doesn't like waiting at the doctor's office."

"She's welcome to stay. I have to be at the beauty parlor at ten. But my new television can keep her company."

"We appreciate that Miz Miller," I say.

"Baby Heart, come here for a minute. I want to show you something before you go."

I follow Miz Miller into her bedroom. She gives me a worried look and says, "I know what you and Bobby Joe are up to. Ya'll be careful." Then she hugs me tight.

With not a minute to spare, I dash down the steps and into the car. Gray's Crossing is twenty miles away. It will take forty-five minutes to get there and I don't want to waste one precious moment of our time together.

My foot is heavy on the gas pedal as I speed along the two- lane country highway between Marysville and Gray's Crossing. I count under my breath to calm myself down, easing up off the gas as I reach fifty. It won't do to be pulled over by the sheriff and get a ticket. John El would find out and demand to know where I was going.

A sign, that would be lit up if it were dark, reads Brown's Motel. It's a long el-shaped one story building, dark gray with peeling white paint trim. But it looks beautiful to me because I can feel his presence.

Blood is pounding in my ears and my heart is beating fast as I enter the motel driveway on two wheels, kicking up gravel. I pull all the way around to the back. A drape opens slightly while I scan the windows. I watch closely as it opens a little wider and see him standing there.

I jump out of the car and run through the backdoor with a kerchief covering my hair, eyes concealed by dark sunglasses and my head down. A room door cracks partially open. I run to it like a starving child runs toward food. The door opens wider then closes behind me. I fall into his arms, and this small room with its' dull green paint, a musty smell and a bed that many secret lovers before us have shared becomes our Garden of Eden for a day. A day we will never forget.

His scent is sweet but in a manly way. It's a natural clean scent like the woods in autumn or the earth after a spring rain. We hold each other and kiss long and deep, trying to make up for three months of being apart and a future without each other. Not a word is spoken as we undress and make our way to the bed.

He begins to put on a rubber. I reach over and take it out of his hand.

"Why did you do that?" He asks.

"Because I don't want anything between us."

"Baby Heart, I have to protect you. You could get pregnant."

My stomach is still flat, so he doesn't know. "That's not possible." I tell him.

"What do you mean?"

I turn my head. I don't want to see the look on his face when I say, "I'm already pregnant."

He turns my face to his and cups my chin in his hand. "Are you sure you want to go through with this?"

"I'm sure, if you still want me."

"I want you, baby and all. I wish both of you were mine."

We make love for a long time. I discover the difference between making love and full-filling my wifely duties. We fly away to another planet, watch starbursts, and feel volcanoes, hot with pressure, erupt. I know what it feels like to be in Paradise, if only for a day.

Bobby Joe pulls potato chips and two bottles of cherry coke from a bag he brought with him and had left sitting on the scarred round wooden table in the room. He opens the soda with a bottle opener that he thoughtfully had packed in the bag. The soda fizzes and foams over onto the table. It got warm while we were heating up the room with our lovemaking.

We sit at the little round table and talk while we snack. I have a towel wrapped around me. It seems like the most natural thing in the world to be with him like this. We both seem older and more serious. He's matured a lot in a few months. And I'm a woman now.

"I remember the first time I laid eyes on you. I thought you were the prettiest girl I had ever seen. I still do. It was love at first sight." He chews potato chips and takes a swallow of soda, as he talks never taking his eyes off me.

We keep our eyes focused on each other, etching every facial expression, every word and every movement in our memories. Our eyes and minds are taking pictures and recording words that float from our mouths on the air — images and comments that time cannot erase.

"Yeah. I remember you saved me from a fight with a bunch of girls who didn't care for me on my first day of school at Marysville High."

"Right. But then they all became your friends."

"Mainly because of you, Bobby Joe."

"You know you were supposed to be my queen at the homecoming parade this year."

"I know. Who would've thought on the first day we met that I would be married and expecting a baby and you would be on your way to the army by the time school started the next year."

"Life throws us curve balls some times," he arches his arm and aims at the trash basket in the corner. The remains of our lunch land like perfect basketball shots.

Then he pulls me into his arms, "Baby Heart, I want to feel you close to me one more time. And when our time together is over, I don't want you to look back with regrets and cry. I want you to remember what we had, what we felt for each other if only for a short time. Nobody can take that from us. When you think of me and this day, I want you to feel joy and know that you were loved and always will be."

It's one-thirty when I get back to Miz Miller's to pick up Rosie Petunia.

"Did old Doctor Scott make you sit there all this time while he waited on the white patients who came in after you?" Rosie Petunia asks with a frown.

"Yeah, something like that." I answer Rosie Petunia as I pry her away from the television set and rush her out of the house.

"What did you find out? Are you in the family way?" she asks after we're in the car heading home.

"Yep, I sure am," I say with a smile. The smile on my face has nothing to do with the baby growing inside of me.

She gives me a funny sideways look, "Well, I guess John El will be happy. He wants to keep you pregnant. He thinks that'll keep other men away from you."

Maybe I think it's a funny look that Rosie Petunia is giving me because I'm feeling a little guilty.

"We better hurry up and get home. We'll both have the devil to pay if I don't have John El's dinner ready when he comes home at three," Rosie Petunia grumbles.

I give her a reassuring look. "You don't have to cook. I'm gonna stop by Brook's Open Pit on the way home and pick up some barbeque, Brunswick stew, coleslaw and that good yellow barbeque sauce that you love, for dinner. He may even have some hush puppies cooked."

Rosie Petunia's round face breaks into a big smile. "Mr. Brooks pulls that pig up out of the ground around two. That meat is gonna be hot, tender and fresh." She smacks her mouth at the thought.

"That's one of my favorite dinners, too," I tell Rosie Petunia.

"This here's been one of the best days in my life. That television is somethin' else. I wish you coulda seen all them stories I watched." She breaks into a long description of what she saw.

This is the sweetest day in my life, I think. I relive my day in Paradise while she rambles on about soap operas she saw on television as I drive towards White Chalk.

By the time we get the barbeque dinners and start on the final leg of our journey home it's 2:45 in the afternoon. As I come to the fork in the road and bear to the right up the hill to our house, I see John El's truck in front of me. My happy state of mind quickly changes to fear. Some men claim they can tell if their wives have been with another man; they can detect the scent of him on her body.

Though I wish I could keep Bobby Joe's scent on me forever, I washed carefully before we left the motel.

"Rosie Petunia," I try to sound calm. "Remember not to tell John El about my visit to the doctor. I want to surprise him."

"I ain't tellin' John El nothing. I'll be too busy enjoyin' my barbeque."

John El is waiting outside the truck when we pull in the yard and park beside him. He eyes me suspiciously. "Where ya'll been?" He drawls it out long and slow, while his green eyes crawl up and down my body. Can he see Bobby Joe in my eyes, I wonder. I lower my head.

Scared to death, I hold my breath to keep the fright out of my voice as I tell him a half truth, "We thought you might like barbeque for dinner. So we went over to Brooks just when he would be pulling the pig out of the ground."

The appetizing smell of the barbeque comes through the bag making it hard for him to stay angry. He smiles, walks over and places his hand on my tummy. "Ain't that just like my little Baby Heart? Thinkin' about me while she's carryin' my seed. How's my little bun in the oven doin'?"

"Let's eat before the food gets cold," I say, moving his hand from my stomach and watching as the light bulb goes off in Rosie Petunia's head. She's a little slow but she isn't stupid.

The next morning over our breakfast coffee, she looks me up and down before she says, "I thought he didn't know and you wanted to surprise him. You didn't go to the doctor yesterday, did you?"

"It's really none of your business where I went." I reply defensively.

"Maybe. But it sho is John El's bitniz," she says mimicking the way he pronounces business.

I remain cool in a show of strength. "So what are you going to tell him?"

"I was just thinkin'. It sure would be nice to have one of them television sets like Miz Miller's got."

"They cost a lot. And getting reception way out here would raise the price even more."

"John El will get anything you want. Ask him for a television set. If he gets it, I will forget how long you stayed at the doctor's yesterday or that we even went to Marysville."

I don't trust her anymore. What else will she want after the television set? But I'm in no position to refuse. "I'll ask him," I say before I turn and leave the kitchen.

Nobody knows what it's like to let someone make love to you that you despise unless they've been through it. My flesh crawls whenever John El touches me. But I'm married to him so I must submit. I feel like I'm cheating on Bobby Joe every time I get in bed with my husband and when I think about Bobby Joe while I'm with John El, I feel bad because I committed adultery. That's one of the biggest sins in the Bible— right up there with murder. If John El ever finds out, he will send me straight to hell.

Sometimes the only way I can get through my duties with John El is to bring my last day with Bobby Joe up on the screen of my mind and listen to him saying, 'I don't want you to regret our last day together. Look back on it with joy and know you were loved and always will be.'

I will never forget Bobby Joe Miller, but his memory must be pushed to the back of my mind if I'm to feel any peace.

MY SISTER IRENE

Irene didn't come to church Sunday and I remember that she looked worse than usual the last time I saw her. It's almost time for her to deliver the baby she got pregnant with the day after Christmas when she and Willie Lee made up. She's on my mind so much! Today I feel like I have to see her, despite John El's rule not to visit my relatives.

I remember our close childhood together.

On cloudy days, Irene and I would stand outside looking for images in the clouds.

"Look, Baby Heart, do you see him? Look right there," she would point to the sky until I followed her finger to the spot where a man with a long pointed chin and beard lay among the clouds.

"Do you see that big bear, Irene?" When she found him we would hold hands watching until he was covered from sight by other clouds.

We did our chores together — bringing in wood for the stove and fireplaces, cleaning the lamps — filling them with kerosene and lighting them to hold back the dark curtain of night.

Irene is still my closest and favorite sister. I can't turn my back on her. I feel like she needs me right now. I pack a bag of food and call Rosie Petunia. "Come and go with me over to Irene's."

She answers me sullenly, "You know John El don't allow you to go visitin'."

Rosie spends every spare moment looking at the new television, even though the reception is so poor she's watching snow and rolling black lines most of the time.

"He didn't say I couldn't go. He just said you have to go with me, Rosie Petunia."

"Well, I don't feel like goin'. I'm tired and I want to watch my story."

"Suit yourself. But I'm going to see about my sister. I don't care what you or John El says."

When I get to her house, Irene is lying on a soiled and sagging shuck filled mattress. Her cheeks are sunken and her skin looks ashen and lifeless. Charley Boy is sitting by her bed holding a wet cloth to her head. Camilla, her oldest daughter who is six now, comes over and stares at me with big, sunken eyes.

"What's wrong with Irene?" I ask Charley Boy.

"Mama's been in bed sick for about a week, ever since Daddy kicked her in the stomach."

Irene moans softly with her eyes closed. I kneel down beside her. A bad odor from her body rises to my nostrils. It smells like rotten meat or something dead. "Where you hurting, Irene?" She places her hand on her stomach.

"Charlie Boy, can she talk?"

"She ain't said nothing since Daddy kicked her in the stomach. She stopped eatin' about two days ago. I can get her to sip a little water."

"Why didn't you come for me or Papa Joe?"

"Too far to walk to yo' house. Besides, we been told none of yo' folks allowed there. Papa Joe is workin' hard, trying to harvest the last of his crop. I didn't want to worry him. And Aunt Rose is workin'."

"Where is Willie Lee?"

"I run him off with the rifle when he kicked Mama. He ain't been back since."

"Charley Boy, you got to help me get Irene in the car so we can take her to the doctor."

We lift her frail body with the baby sticking straight up in her stomach like a hard watermelon— and get her into the car somehow. We load the other children in. Camilla and James stand in the back where their mother is stretched out on the seat. They all look hungry.

The bag of food is still in the car. "Camilla, look in that bag and pass the food out for you and the other kids." I hear them tearing into the cold fried chicken and bread like they haven't eaten in days. Two year old Cherub sits in the front, between Charley Boy and me. She's dirty. Her stomach is sticking out although she is thin with big eyes. I feel guilty about this. I've been living in the lap of luxury, eating anything I want, and driving a big car while my sister is being beaten and starved along with her children.

When we reach Doctor Scott's clinic that serves as the only hospital in Marysville, I pull the car up close to the entrance, hop out and poke my head in the door to the waiting room for colored. "Can somebody come help me get my sister inside? She's too sick to walk."

The waiting room is filled but they all look too sick to help. Just then a young colored man wearing a green jacket that has "Orderly" written on it enters the room. I ask him if he will help me. He finds a wheelchair and brings it to the car. Irene keeps sliding out of the chair. Charley Boy and I hold on to her while the orderly goes back inside and returns with a stretcher. We help him get her on it, and then we all trail behind him into the waiting room.

We sit there ignored for a long time. Finally the colored nurse who works only with colored patients comes into the room. I remember her. She's pretty and haughty. I run over to her and say "We need help right away. My sister is bad off sick."

The nurse—her name is Julia— is wearing a white nurse's cap, white starched uniform and white shoes. Everything I dreamed of being and wearing. She looks at Irene's children with an air of dread. She's probably worried that they may touch her clean uniform with their grimy hands.

"What's wrong with her?" Nurse Julia asks.

"She's pregnant. It's almost time for her to deliver."

"Well, is she in labor?"

"I don't think so. But her husband kicked her in the stomach last week and she hasn't been able to get out of bed since. She stopped eating and talking and just moans."

Nurse Julia walks fast over to the stretcher where Irene is lying very still and moaning. When Julia gets close to her she holds her nose and backs away. "I'll get Dr. Scott. I think her baby may be dead," she whispers to me before she runs from the room.

The orderly returns and starts wheeling Irene away. I ask him where he's taking her and he says, "to the examining room." We sit there worried and waiting. I hold Cherub on my lap and rock her to sleep.

Almost an hour later, Dr. Scott comes into the room. I can't help thinking how much he looks like John El and Rosie Petunia. "Are you Irene's sister?" he asks me.

"Yes Sir," I say snapping to attention, worried about what he will say next. I don't think it will be good because he has a frown on his face.

"She should have been here a week ago. It's too late to save the baby, but we can operate on her to remove it and try to save her life. I need permission from her husband to perform surgery."

I wring my hands in astonishment. "Dr. Scott, her husband kicked her in the stomach. That's why she's in this condition. Anyway, we don't know where he is. Can I sign for the operation?"

"No. Where is her father? He can sign."

"It'll take an hour to go back to White Chalk to get Papa Joe and bring him back. Why can't I sign?"

"It's the law. Either her husband or father if the husband can't be found."

"Doctor, she may die while we're getting him."

He shoots me a stern look. "She may die while you're standing here arguing with me."

I gather up the children and we hurry back to the car. All the way to the country, I pray. It's noon when we get there.

We find Papa Joe in the kitchen getting his dinner so he can eat and return to the field after the sun moves farther west. When I tell him about Irene, he hangs his head and cries. I think he cries all the way to Marysville as he mutters under his breath about finding Willie Lee and tanning his worthless hide.

"Let's just try to save Irene first. We'll take care of Willie Lee later," I say.

I burn up the highway between White Chalk and Marysville. Even with going eighty miles an hour, it's one-thirty when we get back. Then we wait another ten minutes for someone to bring Papa Joe the form that he scrawls his X on.

We sit in the waiting room teary-eyed and worried. I see Julia come in the room and I run over to her. "What are they doing with my sister? Can we see her?"

Julia stares at me from under arched eyebrows like I'm crazy. "You may not see her. They're prepping her for a Caesarian section."

"A what?" Papa Joe asks.

"That's the procedure used to open her womb and take the baby out. That's what you signed the paper for them to do." She looks at us like we're retarded or very dumb people.

"May I use the phone to call my husband? He'll be coming home soon and won't know where I am," I say. My hands are trembling from the nervousness of waiting to see what will happen to Irene and what will happen to me when John El gets home and finds out I left without his permission, unaccompanied by Rosie Petunia.

Nurse Julia shakes her head, "Of course not. This is a doctor's office. We can't have visitors tying up the phone."

I wonder what John El will think when he comes home and finds me gone off by myself. If Rosie Petunia tells him I went to Irene's he might go to her house looking for me and then to Papa Joe's, I think.

Worry about your sister, I tell myself. If I hadn't been such a coward — so afraid of John El, I could've helped her before she got in this condition. If John El beats me for taking care of my sister, I'll just have to take it. He'll be mad but I don't really think he will kill me over this. I sit there holding Papa Joe's hand trying to be strong for him and the children.

It's after five o'clock when the doctor comes into the room. He looks at Papa Joe with a sad face and says, "I'm sorry, but we lost her on the operating table."

Papa Joe turns his tear streaked face to me and asks, "What did he say, Baby Heart?"

I hold him close and tell him, "Irene's gone home with Mama Lilly and Jesus, Papa Joe."

The children hear me. The older ones start wailing. Cherub wakes up looking bewildered and starts crying. She doesn't really know what's happening. I think she's crying because we're crying.

When we get back to White Chalk, I stop at the store where I'm sure I'll find John El. He's sitting on the porch, fanning and looking hotter than a firecracker on the fourth of July. He rushes over to the car before I can get out. The window is down. He leans in, scans my passengers and asks loudly, "What in the hell is the meaning of this, woman?"

"I just lost my sister. Irene is dead. I've been all day getting help for her. I took her to the doctor. They operated on her and she died on the table." Tears are streaming down my cheeks.

"I'm sorry. I didn't know," he says looking sincerely sad. It always strikes me as strange how folks can be so mean to other people while they're living. But soon as they die, they're sorry. He wasn't sorry when he refused to have Irene in our wedding because he said her black eyes and bruises were unsightly. He wasn't sorry when we threw good food to the dogs that would have kept her and her children fed. I wasn't allowed to give them a scrap of leftovers from our table. Now, he's sorry.

I look at him with a steady gaze, "John El, I have to tell my sister Rose. We need to get word to Lincoln, Roosevelt and the others."

"I understand. Use the phone to make calls and go on over to Rose's in the car."

"The children are going to need somewhere to stay," I tell him. There's a question mark in my eyes. I'm hoping he'll say they can all stay with us.

"Why can't they stay with their daddy?" he asks.

"We don't know where Willie Lee is."

"That nigger ain't never been worth a shit," John El spits the words out.

"Not in front of the kids, John El. We'll talk about it later."

He looks over at Cherub sleeping in Papa Joe's lap. "You can bring that one home with you. She's sho nuff got some pretty hair. Those boys need to stay with Joe and help him in the fields."

When Lincoln finds out what happened to Irene, he's furious and goes hunting for Willie Lee the next day with his pistol in his pocket and a rifle across his shoulder. When he can't find him, he goes to the sheriff.

I go with Linc and sit quietly as he explains to Sheriff Russell that Willie Lee killed our sister and we want him arrested.

"Did you witness the murder?" Sheriff Russell asks through a cloud of cigarette smoke.

"No Sir. But all of her children saw him kick her in the stomach."

"I don't think you want to put her children through takin' the stand against their own daddy even if the judge allows it."

"Maybe you don't understand," Lincoln says. I can tell Linc's getting hot under the collar. "My sister is dead. Are you saying we should let him get away with it?"

"Either that or take care of it yourself. The court doesn't see much sense in getting mixed up with fights between husbands and wives. If I went out there and arrested him, I doubt if they'd bring him to trial. And if they did and the children testified, that still won't prove that the kick in the stomach killed her." He dismisses us with an air of indifference even though he says he's sorry.

On our way home Lincoln says, "I don't know why I wasted my time with that cracker. They hardly bring charges against a white man for beatin' or killin' his wife. When colored folks are involved, they care even less."

"So I guess a woman is just her husband's property to do with whatever he wants." I shiver as a cold chill runs down my spine.

"Yeah. I know what I have to do," Lincoln says calmly with a frown. "You heard him. If I kill Willie Lee, they won't arrest me either."

"I think we should go to the funeral home and make arrangements. Forget Willie Lee," I say gloomily.

ANOTHER FUNERAL

SEPTEMBER 13, 1947

On a gloomy day in September we lay my sister Irene to rest in the red Georgia clay. The skies are gray and overcast as we gather around the open grave while the casket is lowered into the ground.

"Dust to dust. Ashes to ashes," the minister says as he sprinkles clods of dirt on the casket.

My eyes are almost swollen shut from crying. The children have cried themselves dry. Camilla twists the hem of her new dress. I see anger mixed with pain and grief in Charley Boy's eyes. I hold Cherub by the hand. At two she just wants it to be over. She keeps saying, "I want my mama." She doesn't understand that her mother is never coming back.

Out of the corner of my eye, I see a bush move at the edge of the cemetery. Lincoln sees the movement at the same time and takes off running.

We all hear Willie Lee crying and hollering, "Don't kill me! I loved Irene. That's my wife ya'll buryin'."

Lincoln left his pistol and rifle at home in respect for the dead. But he beat the shit out of Willie Lee with his fists. Linc wipes his hands off on his pants and walks back to the gravesite without uttering a word. The minister finishes the burial ceremony, and we all go home with Papa Joe.

John El even comes with us. I start thinking that he's not all bad. Maybe I do have a good husband. He never beats me. Sometimes he puts me across his lap and pretends to spank me like a little girl but that's part of the way he makes love—foreplay as they say in the books I read. I don't care for it, but he never hurts me.

He paid for new clothes for all of Irene's children to wear to the funeral. He says Cherub can live with us and we'll raise her like our own. I decide right then and there that I'm going to treat John El better.

I place my hand on my stomach. I'm mindful of the baby inside and really worried about birthing it after what just happened to Irene. I lean against John El for support. He seems to like that and pulls me closer to him. I feel like I'm making a family now. I'll have two children, including Cherub, by the time I'm sixteen. But I swear to myself that will be all. When this baby comes, I'll find a way to keep from having more.

Charley Boy and James move in with Papa Joe. Camilla goes to live with my sister Rose. I wish I could keep all the children together.

They've lost so much — Mama Lilly, Irene and now each other. I tell them not to worry; they'll see each other at least once a week. Rose and I plan to get all the children together on Sundays after church for dinner at her house. I'll bring the food. The children will get to see each other and run and play.

It's okay with John El as long as we go elsewhere. He doesn't want children playing in our house — afraid they may mess up the fine furniture.

We will take them to the cemetery once a month to visit their mother's grave and carry flowers.

"I will make sure they never forget you, Irene," I say, looking toward the cloudy sky for our bear.

24

CHERUB

John El has a whole new outlook on life since Cherub came to live with us. Sometimes I think he likes that baby more than me. When he comes home for dinner every day, I hear him bellowing, "Cherry, Cherub. Where is my sweet little Cherub?"

Usually she meets him at the door with outstretched arms. He lifts her up and nuzzles his face in her soft light brown ringlets or tosses her up in the air as she giggles. Sometimes she hides behind the door or furniture, and he runs around looking for her until she sneaks up behind him, laughing out loud at their game.

I'm happy—at least most of the time— that they take to each other so well. Every now and then when I see the look that crosses his face when he strokes her hair, I wonder where I've seen it before. And one day an old memory comes back of me, when I was a little older than

Cherub, toddling into the store and John El stroking my hair with his green eyes wide and glistening. The memory troubles my mind for a short while then I brush it aside and get back to what I was doing, content with the notion that John El will make a good father to his own child.

I love Cherub. Having her with me has made me happier. I'm glad that she will soon have a playmate when my baby comes. She calls me Aunt Baby Heart. At first she called me Mama. I stopped that. I always want her to know Irene was her mama. Irene had so little in life. I want to keep her memory alive, make sure her children know about her even if Cherub is too young to remember.

JOEL — MY FIRST BORN

MARCH 1948

Before day on March 12, 1948, a pain like nothing I've ever felt before rips through my stomach. I know the time I've both feared and looked forward to is here.

"John El!" I scream and poke him in his boney back.

He rolls over, sits up in the bed and rubs the sleep out of his eyes. "What's the matter?" He asks.

"The baby is coming. I just had a labor pain."

John El jumps out of bed, pulls on his jeans and is half way out the door before I call out to stop him. "Where're you going?"

"To take you to the doctor."

"In case you haven't noticed, I'm still in bed."

"Well get the hell out of bed and put on some clothes. We don't have time to waste."

"John El, the doctor said we should time the pains and come in when they get about five minutes apart."

"Five minutes apart, my ass. As far as we have to go over these bumpy roads, we may not get there on time as it is."

"Then, you'll just have to go get the mid-wife or let Rosie Petunia deliver the baby."

"Are you crazy? I wouldn't let that drunken mid-wife or Rosie Petunia touch my baby. I'll wake Rosie up while you get on some clothes. She'll take good care of Cherub while you're in the hospital."

I start putting on my clothes and another pain strikes. When it passes over and I catch my breath, I say "Yeah. She's moody with me but I can trust her with Cherub. She's almost as fond of her as you are."

I grab the little overnight bag that I've kept packed and sitting by my bed for the last week and we hurry out to the car. Between pains on the way to the hospital in Marysville, I tell John El that I want to name the baby Joel if it's a boy.

"That's a fine name," he agrees. "I like that. It combines my name and yo's. Jolee and John El – Joe El."

I nod my head, happy that he agreed, although I didn't have either one of us in mind when I decided on the name. I was thinking more of Bobby Joe and Papa Joe. "I hope people won't drag it out by calling him Joe El. His name will be Joel," I say firmly.

"Don't matter what they call him. He'll soon be working in the chalk mine with me. They'll have two of us, John El and Joe El" he says with a sly annoying wink.

It's still dark when we get to Dr. Scott's Clinic that also serves as a hospital. The door is locked. John El bangs for about five minutes before a sleepy orderly appears and lets us in. He says only three or four patients are in the hospital and the nurse is taking care of them. John El is upset and hollers at him, "My wife is having our baby. Where is the doctor?"

"At home in bed, I suppose. It's five in the morning," the orderly answers sullenly.

"Then you better call him and tell him to get over here," John El shouts.

"That's not my job." The orderly yawns.

John El grabs his arm before he can walk away. At the same time I have a sharp labor pain, double over and scream loud enough to wake the dead. This brings the nurse hustling into the waiting room. She grabs a clipboard and starts asking a string of questions: "What's your name? What's your address? What's wrong with you? Who is the baby's father?"

My husband interrupts her. "This here is my wife, Miz John El Murphy. So that would make me the baby's father. Cut out all this nonsense and get Dr. Scott over here before she drops the baby on the damn floor."

The nurse, who is white, peers at John El who looks paler than usual, and says with her hands on her hips, "It's against the law for a white man to marry a colored woman in Georgia."

"I ain't no white man. But Dr. Scott is my uncle and if you don't call him right now, you're gonna be lookin' for another job tomorrow." John El turns red from anger.

A blush starts at the base of the nurse's neck and runs up to her forehead. I'm sure she's never had a colored man speak to her like this before. She starts to say something then seems to think better of it and picks up the phone instead.

After she speaks to Dr. Scott on the phone, she calls the orderly and says curtly, "Take this patient down to the colored section in the basement and show her to a bed." She shoots John El an evil look and walks away.

By nine that morning my baby boy is in my arms. I look at him with disappointment. I imagined my baby was a boy but I always visualized him as having brown skin and looking like me. Instead, this baby is light skinned with green eyes. He's a tiny duplicate of John El.

Later when I place my baby to my breast, love flows with the milk and it no longer matters what he looks like. He's my son!

John El is beside himself with pride and joy. He keeps saying, "Hot damn! I made a boy. He looks just like me."

 26

TEN YEARS LATER

1958

Ten years have passed since my son was born. I have a daughter who came in May of 1949, a year after Joel. I swore I wasn't going to end up like Mama Lilly and Irene with a baby every year. So I learned a way to stop getting pregnant without John El being any the wiser.

We're one big happy family. I seldom think about Bobby Joe anymore. When I do, he seems unreal —like a beautiful dream I had a long time ago. Cherub is 12, Joel is 10 and my May Lilly is 8. She was named after the month she was born and Mama Lilly. Raising my children keeps me busy.

Now that they are older and in school most of the day, I have joined a book club that sends me a new book through the mail once a month. I read novels and other books that take me to far away places. Frank Yerby is my favorite novelist. He's a colored man born and raised in Augusta, Georgia. I feel like I know him. Most of his books are about white folks in the Ante-bellum South. I like reading "A Woman Named Fancy" even though she's a southern white aristocrat being served by my ancestors. It's like being in another time and place while I enjoy the romantic story.

I don't go anywhere without the kids. John El doesn't seem jealous of other men noticing me any more. Now that I'm a mother of three kids and twenty-seven years old, he seems to think I'm an old woman. He pays more attention to Cherub than he does to me, which is a concern. I'm not jealous. It just doesn't seem right.

Cherub was a beautiful baby and she's growing into a gorgeous young woman. She looks a lot like me when I was her age, with rich bronze skin. Her hair, unlike mine, is sandy and it hangs in heavy ringlet curls. Her eyes are just like Irene's, an amber color that gives the appearance of liquid. Put all that together with her heart shaped face and she's one pretty little girl. That can be more of a curse than a blessing.

An old woman looks at her one day and says to me, "That one can spend any man's money when she gets a little older."

I tell the woman loud enough for Cherub to hear, "She's not being brought up to depend on men to take care of her. She's going to get a good education and be able to take care of herself."

In 1949, a week before she was to come into her inheritance, Rosie Petunia died. We found her dead in her bed one morning. I still feel bad about that. She was always looking forward to her freedom and owning half of everything. I never let on to John El that she shared their secret with me.

I want to trust my husband but sometimes a shadow of doubt crosses my mind about John El when I think about how Rosie Petunia died suddenly just before she would have come into half of his estate and how he looks at Cherub and still wants to hold her on his lap even though she's going on thirteen. I put a stop to that. Neither one of them likes it but I put my foot down and said she's too big to sit on his lap.

One thing is for sure; all of the children love their daddy. He spoils them rotten with candy and all kind of goodies from the store, new clothes and anything else they want. He never whips them either. I have to do all the discipline and spanking when they need it.

They would rather be with their daddy. But that's okay with me. I know children have to be raised up right. They love me too and will appreciate it one day.

Now that he's ten Joel spends a lot of time at the store and chalk mine with his daddy. Says he's learning the business so he can take it over when he gets grown. I make sure he goes to school. I tell him I want him to finish high school and go to college so he can learn how to run the businesses better than his daddy and above all improve things at the chalk mine so it will be safer and better for everybody's health.

I'm trying to raise my son to be kind and considerate of other people. I can't change John El but I hope and pray that Joel doesn't become hard like him.

Papa Joe quit sharecropping and moved to Sawyersville to live with Lincoln about a year after Irene died. Charley Boy and James went back home to live with Willie Lee. Papa Joe wanted to keep the boys with him but Willie Lee wouldn't here of it. Charley Boy ran off and joined the army as soon as he turned seventeen. James is working with his daddy making moonshine. He dropped out of school after fourth grade and is following in his daddy's footsteps to my sorrow. Camilla is happy with Rose. She will stay with Miz Miller so she can start high school in town next year.

 *27*

EASTER 1958

It's the Saturday before Easter. John El presses a wad of twenty-dollar bills in my hand before he leaves for work at the store. "Take the kids to town and buy them some pretty Easter clothes." He reconsiders and hands me what I think is another twenty. I look at it and it's a one hundred dollar bill. "Get something extra special for Cherub and a pretty dress for yo'self."

I smile and say, "Thank you. With this much money, I may drive all the way to Atlanta and shop at Davison's or Ritchie's."

"I don't care if you do. Just drive careful. I want my wife and children to be the best dressed family in White Chalk and Marysville on Easter Sunday."

After he leaves, the children and I get dressed for our shopping trip. We're all light headed and giddy with happiness. The children have been to Atlanta before but we don't go there often. I pack a picnic lunch including a jug of lemonade and a jug of water. I put towels and blankets in the trunk of the car along with the food. "We'll stop along the road on the way back and have a picnic," I tell the children.

I prefer to have a picnic so we don't have to drive around Atlanta looking for colored restaurants. I try to spare my children from having to go to the colored side in white restaurants or to the colored drinking fountains.

It's hard for me to answer their questions about why colored folks can't sit and eat in certain places or drink from certain water fountains. I don't want them getting the notion that they're not as good as white folks.

I also have to be careful at home. Because their daddy owns every thing, I don't want them growing up thinking that they're better than everybody else, white and black.

The sky is clear blue as we pile into the car. The sun is warm. Easter lilies sway in the gentle breeze on long green stems. I thank God for my blessings and try to ignore the nagging fears created by my mother's warnings when I was a child.

Mama Lilly would say, "Baby Heart, if you get too happy in the mornin', you're gonna cry before nightfall." Or she would say sometimes, "Too much pride ain't good for you. The prideful fall hard."

A chicken hawk circles overhead, I know that means bad luck for the chicken it's looking for. But Mama Lilly had an omen for that to. "A circlin' chicken hawk means somebody is gonna die."

Joel, who's always hungry because he's a growing boy, asks, "Mama, what if we get hungry before we get to Atlanta, can we eat a sandwich?"

"Boy, you just finished eating breakfast." I say.

"Riding makes us hungry, Mama," May Lilly chimes in.

"All right. If you get too hungry, we can pull over and eat. But not before we get halfway."

It rained hard last night. The roads are slick with mud. I'm having a little trouble keeping the Cadillac from sliding into a ditch. But I have a good feel for the new baby blue car. I hold it steady, careful not to get stuck.

As I round the final bend in the road before I reach the paved highway, I see a car stuck in the mud. It has a New York license plate. Two men are trying to push it free while another man sits behind the wheel to guide the car. They have on suits, ties and dress shoes. I wonder where they're going all dressed up on Saturday. I come close enough to see their faces and I don't recognize them. I know from the license plate that they don't live around here.

I edge carefully past them and find a spot to pull over without getting stuck myself. I tell the children to stay in the car. I put on the old shoes, that I threw in the car in case I have to walk in the mud, before I get out and holler to the men, "It looks like ya'll stuck pretty bad. Need a push?"

"No ma'am. We wouldn't want you to mess up that pretty new car. We're rocking it. I think we'll get it free any minute now."

They place strong black hands on each side of the rear end and push. The driver presses down on the gas and the car lurches free of the ditch with a powerful surge that sends red mud splattering on the suits and faces of the two men who were pushing.

"Oh, my," I say. "Your suits are full of mud. Where ya'll heading?"

"We're on our way to our sister's funeral in Marysville."

I think about how I felt when Irene died. I feel really bad for them. "Wait a minute," I say. "I have some water and towels in the trunk of my car. I'll try to wash some of that mud off for you."

"We'd appreciate that, ma'am. Hate to go in the church like this."

I run to my car and come back with the water and towels. I sponge as much of the mud as I can off their suits. Then I wet the clean end of the towel and begin wiping mud off the face of one of the men. I'm almost finished when I hear the sound of a truck approaching.

I look up and see John El.

The fury on his face is worse than a raging storm. He brings the truck to a stop and jumps out. "Woman, what in the hell you doin'? Have you been using my new car to push these niggers' car out of a ditch?"

"No," I say humbly and lower my head. "They're on their way to their sister's funeral. I was just trying to help them get some of the mud off so they can look presentable."

John El slaps me so hard my head spins. "Don't lie to me woman. You've been sneakin' around behind my back with this nigger. Why else would you be wipin' his face and standing in front of these men like a strumpet with your hair loose and no scarf on your head."

I hold my hand to my face that feels like it's on fire. "John El, I don't even know these men. I was just trying to help," I plead.

One of the men tries to intervene. "Mister, if this is your wife, I apologize. We don't know her. Like she said, she was just trying to be a Good Samaritan."

This infuriates John El more. He reaches for his gun. I run, screaming to the car.

I have the car door open and I'm halfway in when he catches me. Without a word he aims the pistol at my heart and pulls the trigger. The bullet makes a thudding sound as it enters my chest. I feel pressure, like I've been hit by a ton of bricks. And pain. But I'm able to bend my body and get under the wheel. The key is in the ignition. I turn on the motor and begin to pull away just as I hear another shot.

Joel screams. "Daddy, don't. You shot my leg."

I push down on the gas pedal with all my might. Vroom! The car takes off, kicking mud into John El's face. I clutch my heart with my left hand. Blood streams through my fingers. It has a metallic smell. Screams come from the backseat. My children. Dear Lord, don't let us die here like this. Terror rings in my ears. I don't stop to look for traffic as I speed out onto the highway. All I can think about is getting to the hospital and saving the lives of my children. I don't know if the girls are hurt. I know my son has been shot in the leg. And I think a bullet pierced my heart. But how can I still be alive if I've been shot in my heart?

The car zooms down the highway ninety miles an hour, drifting over the yellow line.

A police Siren sounds behind me. Red lights flash commanding me to pull over. Somehow I guide the car to the side of the road and cut off the engine. Then I slump over the steering wheel as a veil of darkness slowly descends. I'm at peace.

 *28*

SEEKING JUSTICE

I hear a voice saying "I think she'll make it if that bullet doesn't shift. We need to get her to Atlanta where they can perform surgery but I'm afraid to have her moved even by ambulance. Too risky."

My eyes flutter open slowly. I look into Doctor Scott's blue eyes. "Are you awake Jolee?" he asks.

I look around the room trying to figure out where I am and what Doctor Scott is talking about. Then I hear John El's voice. "I'm sure glad she's alive. I didn't mean to hurt her or my son. It was just an accident."

"Things happen between husband and wife, John El. We understand," the doctor says in a kind voice.

A scream comes out of my mouth without me willing it. "Call the police. Get him away from me. He tried to kill me and my son."

"Calm down, Jolee." Doctor Scott pats my hand. "You've got to be quiet and still. We don't want that bullet moving around in your chest. You're lucky it didn't hit a major artery in your heart. You'd be singing with the heavenly choir about now if it had. As soon as we can stabilize that bullet, I want to send you to Grady in Atlanta. They have surgeons there who will know how to remove it and you will be good as new."

"First, I need you to remove John El from near me and call the police." My words come out in a raspy whisper but they are calm and measured. I can hardly believe it's me speaking.

"Baby Heart, you know I didn't mean to hurt you." John El drawls. "I'm beggin' for yo' forgiveness." He reaches for my hand.

I'm scared to death of him and the bullet. I try not to scream. I muster all the strength and calmness that I can, look straight at Dr. Scott and say, "Get him out of here. Call the police, please."

John El gets up from beside my hospital bed and heads for the door. I hear him mumble something as he leaves. I can't understand what he's saying.

Dr. Scott calls for a nurse. When she comes in I hear him tell her to prepare a shot. I need to be sedated.

"I don't want to be sedated. I want the police and I want to see my children. Where is my son? Is he all right? Do my folks know what happened to me?"

"There, there. You're going to be all right just as soon as this medicine gets into your bloodstream," Doctor Scott says, impatience in his voice.

The nurse holds my arm still. I feel a prick from the needle. Then I begin to drift off into a warm fuzzy haze where everything is just fine. I forget about John El and the police while I float above a beautiful green meadow without a worry in the world. From my faraway cloud, I hear Dr. Scott tell the nurse, "That morphine will keep her still and quiet for awhile."

I awake to see a blue uniform hovering over me. I don't know what day it is or what time but I look at his badge and know that he's a policeman.

"I'm sure glad to see you," I say. I'm still groggy from the shot.

He pulls out a notepad and holds a pencil to begin writing. "What happened?"

"My husband shot me and my son. The police brought me here. But I don't think he made a report because my husband was here earlier, instead of in jail where he should be."

"Where did the shootin' take place?" He asks as nonchalantly as if he was asking what I had for breakfast.

"Between White Chalk and Marysville. Just before I got on the highway." My mind is clear now. I draw on all the strength I have because I want to give him the right information.

He closes his pad and says, "I wish somebody had told me before I wasted my time. That's out of my jurisdiction."

"Who should I report it to? If this bullet moves I'm a dead woman. I want the authorities to know what he did before I die."

"You need to call the County Sheriff's Department."

"Will you call for me?" I ask in a whisper that sounds more like a begging whine. I touch the bandages on my chest, beginning to feel the toll again of the weight of a bullet close to my heart.

Begrudgingly, he agrees to stop at the sheriff's office and ask them to send a deputy to take the report.

I drift back off into a fitful sleep. When I wake up again, Papa Joe and Lincoln are sitting by my bed.

I try to raise my head. "Hey, Papa Joe. Hey, Linc."

Papa Joe has been crying, I can tell by the redness of his eyes. Lincoln's eyes are red too but I see anger instead of tears flashing in them.

"I have to kill him. I don't care if they send me to the electric chair. I ain't gonna stand by and see another one of my sisters buried in the cold Georgia clay and do nothing," Lincoln says. He's holding on to one of my hands and Papa Joe has the other one.

"Lincoln, let the law handle this. Someone should be here from the sheriff's office any minute." I tell him.

"What you want to bet they don't do a damn thing. You know what they said when we tried to get help when Irene died."

"I know. But this is different. I can tell them what happened. I have witnesses. He shot Joel, too. Surely they will do something about that."

"We'll see." Lincoln sounds skeptical.

"You're right, Baby Heart. We need to see what the law will do first, Lincoln." Papa Joe looks at Lincoln with pleading eyes.

A little later, the deputy sheriff saunters in. "I'm Sheriff Russell. I hear you want to report a shooting that took place last Saturday over 'round White Chalk."

I recognize him. He's the same cracker we talked to when Irene died. Still I try to give him respect, knowing I'm beholding on him to get any protection or justice. "Yes Sir. My husband shot me and my son."

"Why'd he go and do that?"

"Well, I stopped to help some men who got stuck in the mud on their way to a funeral. I was wiping mud off the face of one of the men when my husband rolled up in his truck. He accused me of carrying on with the men and shot me. Then he pointed the pistol in the back of the car and shot my son in the leg. I don't know why he shot him. He always seemed crazy about Joel."

"What's your husband's name and address?"

"His name is John El Murphy and he lives …"

Before I can finish the sentence Sheriff Russell gets a funny look on his face and shuts his notebook. "Yo' name is Jolee Murphy, right?"

"Yes Sir."

"Well, let me explain somethin' to you, Jolee. The law don't like to get mixed up in domestic disputes."

I can't believe what I just heard. "Officer, this isn't just a domestic dispute. He shot me. Aimed right for my heart. It's a miracle and only through the Grace of God that I'm alive."

"It seems to me that you provoked him. Any man might go out of his mind if he catches his wife wiping on another man's face. I don't know what I would do under those circumstances."

"All I want you to do is arrest him and let the judge and jury figure out if he's guilty."

"You think you're right smart for a colored woman, don't you? Know all about the law, huh?"

"I'm just trying to get the protection due me under the law," I say calmly.

"Alright. I'm goin' out there and arrest him right now. But I bet he'll be out before I go off duty. And I expect you're gonna be in worse trouble for putting him in jail. Sometimes a husband gets real mad about that and kills his wife. If you talk to him instead, ya'll can make up and work things out." He pauses at the door, "Sure you want me to lock him up?"

"Yes Sir, we want him locked up." Lincoln and Papa Joe both say.

"I was talking to her not ya'll."

"Yes Sir, I want him locked up. I'll press charges." My voice is weak but I'm sure with the help of Papa Joe and Lincoln, I can do it.

BACK TO GRADY HOSPITAL

On the long quiet ride to Atlanta in the ambulance, I have time to think. My mind is confused. I don't know what to do, where to turn. If I survive surgery and they remove the bullet, I have a chance to take my children, run away and make a new life. If I die, he will have my kids. That thought makes me want to fight to live. But if I'm left an invalid, I'll have to go back to him. How can I bear looking at John El Murphy for the rest of my life, hating and fearing him with every breath I take?

Linc was right. The law didn't do anything to help me. They didn't even lock him up. There's supposed to be a hearing as soon as I'm able to testify. I know how that will go. As soon as I say I was wiping mud from a strange man's face I will be Jezzie Bell and he the wronged husband.

Actually, the more I think about this maybe it was my fault. I broke all the rules. My hair was loose. No scarf over it. And I touched the face of a strange man. If that didn't justify a shot in the heart, what I did over ten years ago sure did.

I remember the time I spent with Bobby Joe in the motel room like it was yesterday. John El never found out about that. But I know and God knows. Maybe God is punishing me. Maybe I should just go back to John El, beg his forgiveness and forget about leaving him or going to court.

They lift the stretcher with me on it carefully out of the ambulance. I look at the large gray complex that's Grady Hospital and remember the first time I came here hoping to save Mama Lilly's life. I was impressed with how big it was. I watched the doctors and nurses and still hoped that I would one day wear a nurse's starched white uniform and be one of them, caring for the sick. Now those dreams are dead and gone. All I can hope and pray for is to leave here without a bullet lodged close to my heart.

Soon a gaggle of doctors are around my bed, asking questions and examining my chest. Then I'm back on the stretcher heading for the lab. X-ray is the first stop. After the tests, I'm carried back to my room exhausted. A hospital worker brings in a tray of bland looking food with wiggly red Jell-O for dessert. I look at the tray without appetite and push it away.

He comes silently into view and stands with folded hands. He watches, as I lay propped up on the white pillows with the bed raised so I can eat.

"John El, what are you doing here?" I ask listlessly. Too tired to be afraid of him.

"I'm here to see about my wife. I had to come up to be with you if they decide to operate and to pay for the hospital bill." He twists a cap in his hands, his jaw clenching and unclenching.

"That's good of you." I don't know if he can tell I'm being sarcastic. I'm not sure he even knows about sarcasm. It doesn't matter. I just want to rest. I turn my face away from him and pretend to be asleep. I don't know when he leaves because I fall asleep for real.

The next thing I know, the nurses are waking me up for a sponge bath and to get me ready for breakfast. It's a new day. I'm hungry after not having lunch or dinner yesterday. I eat the bland oatmeal and fruit; try to drink a glass of milk. Before I finish, a doctor comes in. He's young and white.

"Good morning, Jolee," he says cheerfully.

"Good morning, Doctor." My voice quivers. I'm nervous, worried about what he's gonna say next.

He clears his throat, pulls up a chair beside my bed and sits down. Strands of straight black hair fall over his forehead. "Jolee, I have the results back from the X-rays and the other tests." He hesitates.

"When will they operate?" I ask. My mind is made up to go through with it so I can live a normal life and take care of my children.

"I'm sorry, Jolee" He sounds really sorry. "But the X-rays show that bullet is too close to the main artery leading to the heart. We can retrieve it but the risk is too great that we may sever or damage the artery and lose you."

The report sinks me into a dark pit of utter despair. "Will I be an invalid for the rest of my life, Doctor?"

"There is no reason that you can't live a normal life. You will need to rest and regain your strength gradually. Don't engage in strenuous physical exercise and don't lift anything over five pounds. We have a tight fitting undergarment that you should wear at all times to bind your chest and keep the bullet from shifting."

Tears stream down my cheeks. I suppose I should be grateful for life and my children. But the thought of returning to spend the rest of my days bound down with John El is almost too hard to accept.

The doctor leaves and the next voice I hear is Lincoln's.

He's alone. I'm glad for that. I need to talk to someone. I need him to help me figure out what I'm feeling, what I should do. Lincoln is the only one I feel comfortable talking about my personal life with. I used to have Candy to help me figure things out but she finished high school and went on to college. When she graduated she moved to Detroit where she teaches now. I miss her and wish she were here to confide in but Lincoln may be able to help me sort out my life and plan for the future.

"Hey, Baby sister. How you feelin'?" He asks leaning over to give me a kiss on the forehead. He's dressed in slacks and a white shirt. I've lost track of time. It must be Sunday or he took off from work.

"I don't know, Lincoln. The doctor just gave me some bad news."

"What bad news? You didn't have the operation yet, did you?"

"No. There won't be an operation. He says it's too risky. I'm going to have to live with this bullet in my chest, so close to my heart that I'm scared with every breath I take that it will shift and kill me."

Linc wipes the tears rolling down my face with his big hand made rough and calloused by long years of cutting trees at the sawmill. "That bastard! Has he been here?"

"Yeah. He came a day ago. Said he had to come to see about me and make arrangements to pay the bill. They're gonna release me tomorrow. I know he'll be back to take me home."

"Baby Heart, you can't go back to him. Next time he'll kill you for sho."

"I don't want to. But I have to. He has my kids. If I leave him, he'll keep my children. Without them I might as well be dead. I won't have anything to live for."

"If you get away from him, you can figure out how to come back and get the kids. If he kills you, you can't help them. That's the way I see it."

"I don't think he'll kill me. He says he's sorry and didn't mean to hurt me."

"You believe that bullshit? How in the hell a man gonna shoot you in the heart and not mean to do it?"

"Like the police said, I provoked him. I had no business stopping to help those men."

"It wasn't wrong of you to help them. You just have a kind nature. You didn't mean no harm. John El did. It wasn't yo' fault, Baby Heart. You gotta stop thinkin' like that or you won't be able to help yo'self or those kids."

"Lincoln, there's something I haven't told you or anybody else." I pause.

"What?"

I'm ashamed to look my brother in the face. I turn my head. "It's hard for me to tell you this. But shortly after I married John El, I committed adultery. He never found out about it. Even though I didn't have anything to do with those men I stopped to help, I feel guilty for what I did long ago. Maybe what happened is the Lord's way of punishing me for my sin."

Lincoln stands up and shakes his head. "I don't go to church a whole lot anymore and I don't read the Bible much but I believe that the Lord has more sense than to punish you like that. You won't nothing but a chil' when you married him. John El took advantage of you and all of us. Don't you think the Lord knows about that?"

Listening to Lincoln helps me to see things more clearly. I also see the danger I'm in. If he did it once, he can do it again. And I may not see it coming. Like this time, I may not know what I'm doing that will drive him over the edge. "Linc, you make lots of sense. But I have to be careful not to make my move too soon."

"Too soon? It looks like you didn't make it soon enough, if you ask me."

"I know what you mean but it won't do to confront him. We have to be smart about this. I'll go home with him, play the obedient invalid wife while I gain strength and make arrangements to leave him — to get as far away from White Chalk as I can and take my children with me."

30

GOING BACK HOME

On the trip home from the hospital there is mostly silence between John El and me. I can't stand to look at him. The sight of him makes my stomach churn. He makes me that sick, angry and worried. I have to ask him about my kids. I keep my face turned to the window. "How are the children?"

He talks slower than usual and so low I have to ask him to repeat what he said several times. "Well, Joel came home from the hospital the same day they took you to Atlanta. He's doin' okay."

"What about May Lilly and Cherub?"

"Willie Lee came and took Cherub home with him. She lives with him now. May Lilly is fine. You remember Ruby Mae who worked in the fields for me. I got her stayin' at the house taking care of May Lilly and Joel."

"Why did you let Willie Lee take Cherub? You know he isn't fit to take care of her."

"I didn't have no say in it. He brought the sheriff to pick her up. They say he's the daddy and I don't have legal right to her. Maybe they'll let her come back when you get well."

I'm about to explode with anger. But I count to ten under my breath, trying to control my racing heart and keep my thoughts to myself. I think about the law; how quick they can take Cherub away from me but can't take John El and lock him up after he almost kills me and shoots his son. I think about how John El has messed up my life and family over nothing. All I can do is sit here and swallow it.

When we pull up to our house, I see May Lilly sitting on the front porch in the big rocking chair with her favorite doll baby cuddled in her arms. Joy moves in my heart— the first happiness I've felt since that awful Saturday two weeks ago.

She runs down the steps and waits while John El helps me from the car.

"Mama, Mama. I'm so glad you're home." She hollers over and over.

"I am too, baby. I want to hug you and kiss you but I can't bend over." A strange look crosses her face like a dark shadow. I think she just realized that things are different; that I won't be able to run and play with her, pick her up and swing her around anymore. So much has changed. I can tell she can't understand it all right away.

"Where is Joel, May Lilly?"

"Inside reading his comic books." She looks up at me intently.

When I get inside the house I call to my son, "Joel, Joel, where are you? Mommy's home."

My poor wounded heart breaks into tiny pieces when I see my son limp slowly toward me. His eyes have deep, dark circles under them. His face seems much older than his ten years. He comes over and takes my hand. "I'm glad you're home, Mama. How you feeling?"

"I'm all right, Son. How're you?"

"My leg doesn't hurt much anymore. Dr. Scott says it's healing well enough for me to go back to school next week. And this summer I'll be well enough to help Daddy at the store and chalk mine."

I nod my head while I think how innocent and forgiving children are and hope we will all be far away from John El and his chalk mine before he can hurt us anymore. I pull my son close to me and hug him. May Lilly fills the circle of my other arm. Only Cherub is missing. My heart aches for her.

John El helps me upstairs without a word. I make my way to the guest bedroom that has never been occupied by a guest. I'm still not allowed company even for a few hours or minutes.

The warm balmy days of spring soon give way to a stifling hot summer. We keep the electric fans blowing on high day and night but all they do is re-circulate the hot air. I've never seen it this hot before. Our ceilings are high and we keep the drapes drawn but nothing cools the house.

The heat saps what little strength I've gained. I spend most of my days sitting on the porch fanning and reading the novels that I receive through the mail order book club I joined years ago. They take me away from White Chalk to big cities and sometimes other countries where men and women of wealth and culture ride in fancy limousines, go to balls and often cross each other in fascinating and unusual ways.

Most of the books I read are about love and romance, causing me to still daydream about Bobby Joe, the great love of my life. I wonder where he is and what he's doing. Sometimes he walks quietly into my sleeping dreams and we make love. The next morning I wake up with a smile on my face.

I don't care much for Ruby Mae, our new housekeeper. She's a large middle-aged dark-skin woman who is sullen and nosey. I admit we need someone to cook, wash and iron, keep the house clean and care for the children but I'm suspicious of her. We could have hired one of my kinfolk who need the money. But my relatives are still barred from the house.

I believe Ruby Mae is also my guard. I'm careful when I talk on the phone and I don't say a word to her or the children about my plans. I talk to Lincoln once a week. We have worked out a code. I'm afraid someone may be listening on the party line or Ruby Mae could pick up the extension phone. Candy's Mama told me a long time ago that Ruby Mae is not to be trusted, that she's dangerous as a rattlesnake.

I have only seen Cherub once since I've been home. My sister, Rose brought her to church last Sunday. Cherub seems more worried about John El than me. She kept asking when she could come home to be with 'Daddy John El.' I'm so worried about her. Willie Lee didn't even let her finish out the school year. I pray I can find a way to take her with us when I escape from White Chalk.

The blistering heat of summer gives away to pleasant autumn weather. The crops have been harvested. I feel new strength surging in my body and spirit.

On the third Sunday in September I sit next to Linc in church. He whispers in my ear —while the preacher is on a high note in his sermon— "Be ready Friday Mornin'. We comin' for you."

"Where're we going?" I whisper back.

"Boston. Don't tell a soul. Make sho you don't let on to the kids. It's best they don't know."

I settle back in my seat and try to concentrate on the rest of the message of the morning being delivered by the preacher but my mind will only grasp Lincoln's message. We're leaving Friday. I have to get rid of Ruby Mae. It won't do for her to be there Friday morning when they come for me. I have to tell Papa Joe goodbye. He's over in Sawyersville.

Maybe I should keep the kids home from school on Friday or plan a way to pick them up without raising suspicion. Then there's Cherub. I don't know how I'm going to steal her away. She doesn't come to school anymore. There's so much to do. My head aches with sadness at the same time it throbs with excitement.

We seem like a normal family as we sit together having Sunday dinner after church. John El is at the head of the table. I'm at the end and May Lilly and Joel sit on either side. Ruby Mae prepared the food before she went home Saturday; roast beef and gravy, potatoes and string beans, homemade rolls and lemonade. There's apple cobbler for dessert.

During dessert, I say to John El, "I think we should cut back on the days Ruby Mae works. I'm getting better and want to start doing more of my own housework."

He frowns and says, "Na. I don't think you're strong enough yet to lift pots and pans and scrub floors."

"I know my feelings better than you. If she takes off on Mondays and Fridays, we'll have enough food left over so I don't have to cook. May Lilly can help with the cleaning. It's time she learned how to take care of a house."

"Well, all right if you sure. When you want me to tell her?"

"Tell her tomorrow not to come Friday and next week she won't come on Monday or Friday."

He frowns as he reaches for a second helping of apple cobbler. "I think we oughta give her at least a weeks advance notice."

"If you're so concerned, pay her for the whole week coming up and give her notice at the same time. That way she'll be happy about getting paid for two days she won't have to work."

"Why you in such a hurry to get rid of Ruby Mae?" His eyes squint in that way of his that lets me know he smells something rotten.

"I'm feeling a lot better. I thought maybe when you come home for lunch Friday afternoon we could have some private time together if Ruby Mae isn't here. The children will be at school." I wink at him.

We haven't slept together, haven't even been in the same bed since I came home from the hospital. I can imagine the wheels turning in his mind.

He smiles, winks back in a knowing way and says in a relaxed drawl "Yeah. I think you're right. We need some private time. Ruby Mae is aroun' too much."

I exhale. One stumbling block removed I think to myself.

Then I say "John El I want to spend the day with Papa Joe Wednesday."

He shakes his head. "You're not able to drive that far yet. Ask Lincoln if he'll bring the old man over here when he gets off work. They can both stay for dinner. That will be nice. I haven't seen Big Joe for a while and I know he wants to see his grandkids."

I'm really surprised. None of my folks have been invited to our house since the wedding eleven years ago. This is amazing. John El is being so nice to me, I begin having second thoughts — do I really want to break up my home and move far away to a big cold city where I have nothing? How will I take care of the kids and myself?

My napkin slides to the floor. I bend over too fast to pick it up and feel something move in my chest. I grit my teeth and hold back a cry. I don't want John El to know. He may insist on keeping Ruby Mae full time. But it reminds me without a doubt why I have to leave.

Lincoln and Papa Joe arrive Wednesday evening before John El gets home from the store. After I greet them and let Papa Joe know how glad we are to see him, I guide Lincoln out back where we're able to talk alone while the children visit with their grandfather inside.

"Don't try to take a whole lot of things. Don't pack nothin' till he leaves the house. What time you think he'll leave?" Lincoln asks.

"He leaves no later than seven, right after breakfast."

"What time the bus come to take the children to school?"

"Seven-thirty. They have to be to school by eight. But I thought I should just keep them home."

"Na. Send 'em on to school. I don't want 'em here when we come for you. We'll pick the kids up from school on the way out. You need to get everything ready between seven-thirty and nine before we get here."

"Lincoln, I'm worried. What are we going to live on up North? I don't want to be a burden on Roosevelt and his family. I don't have any money saved. Everything belongs to John El. I don't even have a bank account in my name. I'm not able to do hard work and I'm not prepared to do anything else."

Lincoln takes a long drag from his cigarette before he speaks. "I heard talk once that John El hides money in his house. You know anything about that?"

"Rosie Petunia told me that he hides money behind a wall in a room that he keeps locked. He's afraid to put it in the bank because he doesn't pay taxes on it. I believe it's true. I hear him nailing in that room sometimes. And when I ask him why he keeps the door locked, he tells me to mind my own business."

"You show us the room Friday. We'll have tools to open the door and tear out the walls. That's yo' nest egg in there."

I shake my head and tremble. "We can't do a thing like that. That's stealing. And if he catches us — if he ever lays eyes on me after he finds out I took his money, what do you think he'll do?"

"I know what he already done for no good reason. You're due that money to support yo'self and his kids. He disabled you. He's got to pay. We can't git help under the law so we have to git it the best way we can. He ain't gonna find you, Baby Heart. Me and Roosevelt got it all figured out. And if he ever comes after me, I got somethin' for him."

"Lincoln, you could never kill anybody. You don't have it in you."

"I guess it seems like all I do is threaten, like I'm weak. I shoulda killed Willie Lee and John El back in the forties then you wouldn't have that bullet close to your heart and Irene would still be alive. I woulda made a little time, maybe a few years. I'd be out by now and we wouldn't be here talkin' about helpin' you run away."

"You're like Papa Joe, Linc. You can't take a life because underneath all of that tough talk you're kindhearted."

"Maybe you're right about me bein' like Papa Joe. I wouldn't kill without a good cause. But I tell you one thing if he tries to hurt you again, I'll snuff his life out same as I would crush a cockroach under my foot."

"What're we gonna do about Cherub, Lincoln? I don't want to leave without her. Maybe you can get Willie Lee to let you take her home with you tonight. Ask him if she can spend a few days with Papa Joe. Then we'll take her with us to Boston."

Lincoln studies the ground and slowly grinds the cigarette out under his heel. "That's a tough one, Baby Heart. If we take Cherub out of the state he can sic the feds on us. Ever since that Lindberg baby was kidnapped, they been real hard on kidnappers. They could give us life. If I had killed Willie Lee, I woulda got maybe a year or two and been out by now. Kidnapping is different."

"But she's our flesh and blood. We're not demanding money or anything. I've been raising her every since Irene died. How can they call it kidnapping?"

"Willie Lee's her daddy. He got all the rights. You see how quick they hauled her off when you went to the hospital. He's got what they call custody. That gives him the right to bring charges. I know how much you love that girl. I love her too. I don't want to see her stuck with Willie Lee. That's why I went to a lawyer. He told me we could be charged with kidnapping if we take her. When she reaches sixteen, she may be able to decide for herself who she wants to live with."

"That's four years from now. She'll be ruined by then." I brush a tear from my eye.

Linc and I hear the rumble of John El's truck coming up the hill at the same time. We hurry inside. I'm putting supper on the table when he comes in the house.

31

FALL 1958

LEAVING JOHN EL AND WHITE CHALK

I toss and turn all night. Don't sleep one wink. Thoughts of leaving, all the things that could go wrong play over and over in my mind like a bad movie. Visions of my new life in Boston, some good, most bad mix in with the running jumble of terrible things that might happen tomorrow morning.

Daybreak and the crowing rooster come as a welcome release. I ease out of bed, wash my face and hands, put on a robe and go downstairs to pack the children's lunches and make breakfast. When Jon El comes down at six o'clock his breakfast is ready. The aroma of brewing coffee and country ham greets him before he enters the kitchen. The children's lunch bags are packed and sitting on the table.

He comes over and puts his arms around my waist. "Good mornin', Baby Heart. Judgin' by the way it looks and smells in here, you're ready to take over."

"See. I told you I'm better. I don't need Ruby Mae as much." A fake smile is spread over my face.

"We'll see what else you ready for when I come home at noon. Matter of fact we can skip lunch." He squeezes me. I hold his arms and pretend to like what he's doing.

After breakfast, he says, "Baby Heart, come give yo' husband a kiss. I'm sorry I hurt you. It's gonna be like old times between us."

I nod agreement and kiss him goodbye. As soon as he's out the door, I wipe my mouth with the back of my hand and hurry upstairs to wake the kids and get them ready for school.

Joel is already up, brushing his teeth. He's an early riser like his daddy. I never have trouble getting him out of bed. He's mature for his age. I decide without giving it much thought that I should tell him we're leaving. He may want to gather some of his favorite things to take with him. And knowing will make it easier, maybe. He's the kind of child who worries a lot and I know how close he is to John El — even after all that's happened.

"Son," I hesitate. "I hope you won't be upset but we're leaving your daddy today." I put my arm around his thin shoulders and hug him.

Joel stares at me with wide eyes. They're hard and cold. He pushes me away. "You're leaving my daddy? Why? Where're you going?"

"Yes, son. You know why. Your daddy loves you and May Lilly but he's a dangerous man. We're going with your uncle Roosevelt to live in Boston."

"Daddy wouldn't of hurt us if you hadn't touched that man. It's not his fault what happened."

"Joel." I try taking a firm approach. "Just tell me if you have special things you want to take with you."

"Don't pack anything of mine 'cause I'm not leaving Daddy. He's showing me how to run the chalk mine, says he's gonna give it to me when I grow up."

"I can't leave you here with him. I would worry myself to death. Don't you remember how it hurt when he shot you? Do you want me to stay here and risk getting killed?"

"Go ahead and take May Lilly with you. I'm gonna stay here with Daddy. I'm not scared of him one bit."

I hear May Lilly get up and head for the bathroom. I don't want to upset her. I whisper to Joel, "Don't mention to anybody what I told you. We're not leaving Daddy. I was just teasing. Finish getting ready for school."

He goes in his room and begins putting on his clothes.

The school bus arrives on time at seven-thirty. I grab their lunch bags and rush them out the door. May Lilly waves goodbye before she climbs on the bus. Joel walks away with a sullen look on his face. He doesn't kiss me goodbye or wave. He's a very intelligent child. I don't know what he's thinking as he climbs on the bus. I have a feeling he didn't believe what I said about not leaving. Uneasiness over what he may do settles in on me.

I bathe, dress and grab a few clothes, toothbrushes and toys that the children may want and stuff them into two suitcases. It's close to nine when I hear a car rumbling up the road. My hands tremble. Fear and excitement mix in my head and run through my body like waves of electricity charging me up. I feel lightheaded and hold on to the bedpost to steady myself.

This is the day that I take back my freedom!

But what will freedom be like if I don't have all of my children with me, If I have no place to call my own and no way to support my family and myself? Will I feel like a fugitive on the run, looking over my shoulder for John El?

I peek out the bedroom window and see a shiny new Oldsmobile rounding the curve to my house. The two packed suitcases are left open on the bed as I rush downstairs to the front door holding my chest so the bullet won't move. The car circles the driveway and pulls across the grass stopping behind the house.

My brother Roosevelt emerges from the driver's seat. I haven't seen him since Irene's funeral. Roosevelt is built closer to the ground than Linc and Papa Joe. He's a big man, wide and sturdy as a brick wall. I wait for them on the porch where they both hug and kiss me. We quickly walk inside to get busy.

"Where's that room you told me about," Linc asks.

"Come on. I'll show you." I take them upstairs to a locked door at the end of the hall.

Roosevelt braces one shoulder against the door, shoves and it gives on the first try. Finding the right place on the wall is not so easy. It looks smooth all over. I look closely and notice what looks like new nail heads in the seams of the knotty pine paneling. "Come here." I call to my brothers. "I believe these are new tacks."

Lincoln takes the crowbar he brought with him and rips a sheet of paneling from the wall. A large square of plaster has been torn out behind the paneling. Carefully wrapped packages are stuffed inside next to the wood frame. Lincoln grabs about ten of the packages and tosses them to me. "Open one." He says.

I remove the brown paper and stare at more money than I've ever seen, all in one hundred dollar bills.

"Put them in your suitcase and let's get out of here," Roosevelt says.

"Aren't y'all gonna fix that wall back?" I ask, shaking with fear of what John El will think and do when he comes home and finds the hole and some of his money gone.

"Hell, No!" Lincoln shouts. "We'll bring yo' bags. You go down ahead of us and make sure the coast is clear. We don't want no surprises like John El waitin' for us."

I stop in my bedroom and stuff the money into one of the bags. I can't get the suitcase shut. I've packed too many clothes and things for the children and I in the two bags. I search for a third suitcase.

Lincoln appears in the bedroom doorway. "What's takin' so long? You not tryin' to count it, are you?"

Roosevelt walks into the room and looks out the window. "Who is that woman I see coming up the road?"

I look and there comes Ruby Mae making her way to my door. "Oh, my God, it's Ruby Mae. She's not supposed to be here today."

"Go git rid of her," Lincoln growls.

She's almost to the front porch when I meet her. "Ruby Mae, what are you doing here? Did you forget you don't have to work today?" I try to sound relaxed.

"Na, I didn't forget. I run outta cigarettes. I'm on my way to the store. Thought I'd stop by to see how you're doin' and if you need anything."

"That's nice of you. I do need some cough drops. I reach in my pocket and hand her a dollar bill."

"The chirren git off to school okay?" she asks, trying to look around me into the house.

"Of course. They left at seven-thirty same as always. I wish you would go on to the store and hurry back. I really need those cough drops." I force a cough.

"That ol' white dust gitting to you, huh?"

"I don't know. Maybe it's just a cold."

Ruby Mae cocks her head to the side and asks, "How you stay wid that man afta what he did to you?"

I know a dog searching for a bone when I see one. I answer sweetly, "My husband is a good man who just made a mistake. Please excuse me. I need to go inside and rest."

She walks on off down the driveway leading back to the road but not before I notice her looking at the tire tracks on the wet grass.

"Linc, Roosevelt, y'all can come on down now." I call to them upstairs.

On a drizzly, overcast fall day I look out the back window of the car at the home I'm leaving behind as we head to the school to pick up my children. All of my eleven years in that house weren't bad. I think about the good times with my children: Cherub, Joel and May Lilly.

There are some pleasant memories of married life too; of times when I thought I had settled in to John El's ways and felt happy and secure being Mrs. John El Murphy, living in the prettiest house in White Chalk high up on a hill where mockingbirds sang and lilacs perfumed the air.

When we arrive at the little church school, I get out of the car breathless and excited. I walk through the open door and scan the classroom for my children. The teacher comes to meet me just as I see May Lilly bent over her desk in the third row near the front, writing.

"Good morning, Mrs. Murphy. Did you come to visit the class today?" The teacher asks with a pleasant smile.

"No, Ma'am. Something has come up and I have to take the children home early."

"I'll get May Lilly for you. But Joel didn't come to school this morning."

My pulse increases rapidly and I feel dizzy. "What do you mean, he didn't come to school? I watched him get on the bus this morning."

"He never came inside. Maybe your daughter knows what happened."

I rush over to May Lilly. "Where is your brother?" I fairly shout. All the other children turn and look at me.

"He ran off through the woods when we got off the bus. I hollered and asked where he was going. I think he said he was going to the chalk mine.

"Come on May Lilly. We have to leave now." I'm real scared. If Joel told John El that I'm leaving, he would have had time to come back home or to the school by now. Maybe he's outside waiting or will cut us off in the middle of the road and start shooting. I don't know what to do except run for our lives and pray. I grab May Lilly's hand and we run out of the door without saying goodbye to the teacher.

"Where's Joel," Linc asks.

"He didn't go inside the school. I think he went to the chalk mine with his daddy."

"Is he in the habit of skipping school to go to the mine?" Roosevelt asks.

"I don't think so. He may have been upset because I told him we were leaving."

Lincoln looks at me with disappointment and disgust in his eyes, "Baby Heart, you promised you wouldn't tell nobody. We talked about not tellin' the kids, remember."

"I know, Lincoln. I'm sorry." I drop my head and let the tears roll.

Roosevelt pushes down on the gas pedal. The tires screech on the gravel driveway as we take off.

May Lilly cries and tugs at my arm. "Mama, where're we going? Did you say we're leaving Daddy? I don't want to leave Daddy and Joel," she screams.

I pull her into my arms. "I don't want to leave Joel or Cherub here either but we have to. As soon as we find our own place I'll send for them."

"What about Daddy? Will he come too?"

"No. It's best for Mama and Daddy to live apart. But we both love you."

"I don't wanna leave my old crazy daddy." May Lilly cries and wails.

Roosevelt can't get up much speed on the rough country road. I keep looking back, expecting John El's truck to come into view. When we reach the fork in the road where we turn right to go to Marysville, Roosevelt turns in the opposite direction. "Why you turning this way?" I ask.

"We have to drop Linc off at his car so he can go back to Sawyersville," Roosevelt says.

"I thought you were going to Boston with us, Linc." My voice comes out whiny like May Lilly's.

"Baby Heart, I wish I could but you know I have to work and see about Papa Joe. Roosevelt gonna make sure you fine."

Linc says goodbye and holds onto my hand for a minute before he gets into his car where he left it parked at the far end of a filling station lot off the highway. As soon as we pull off, I feel his absence. Another missing link in my chain I think, smiling in spite of myself at how the thought fits his name.

Roosevelt seems like a stranger to me. He left home when I was only six. I see him seldom. He used to visit every other summer. He's only been home for funerals in the last ten years. He's much older than me. We're not close like I am with Lincoln.

May Lilly cries herself to sleep as we head back up the highway. Roosevelt isn't much of a talker, I'm glad of that. Soft, soothing music plays on the car radio. I try to sort out my feelings and my fears.

I haven't done much traveling, actually I've never been out of Georgia but I learned a little geography in school. When we pass through Atlanta and follow the signs leading to Chattanooga Tennessee, I figure something's wrong. We're heading north when we should be going east.

From the backseat where I'm still sitting with May Lilly's head in my lap, I voice my concern, "Roosevelt, shouldn't we be going east to get to Boston?"

"Well, I guess now is a good time to tell you. We're not going to Boston. I'm gonna take you and May Lilly to Detroit and then I'll leave for Boston from there."

"Why did y'all tell me we were going to Boston?"

"If you got weak and told somebody, like you did Joel, you couldn't tell them where you were really going 'cause you didn't know. If John EL comes looking for you he'll come to Boston where he can deal with me. The rest is up to you. If you don't want him to find you don't write or call home from Detroit. Don't talk to anybody who might know you from down south."

"How am I gonna keep in touch with Joel and Cherub?"

"Address their mail to me. I'll put it in another envelope and mail it to them. I'll forward any mail you get."

"I don't know anybody in Detroit, Roosevelt. How're you gonna just drop us off there and keep going?"

"Don't you know a girl from White Chalk that you grew up with, named Candy?"

I smile. "Candy! Sure I know Candy. She was my best friend. John El wouldn't allow me to stay in touch with her. She finished high school, went away to college and I didn't hear any more from her."

"She's waiting for you in Detroit. Lincoln made all the arrangements through her mama."

"What if her mama tells someone where we're going?"

"She promised she wouldn't tell a soul. I believe her because she wouldn't want to put her daughter in harm's way."

The thought of being with my friend Candy again brings a little sunshine into this bleak day.

I'm feeling better thinking about being with Candy again until we start going around the mountains. I'd heard about the mountains from people who traveled them coming home from up North. My ears start to plug up and I feel dizzy from the car climbing higher and higher around the sharp curves. I look out the window and it seems like the only thing separating us from our maker is a white picket fence. If the car slides into that thin white railing we could plummet 3000 feet or more, I estimate.

"Roosevelt, you feel okay driving around these mountains?"

"Sure. Ain't nothing to it. I drive through mountains going back and forth to Boston. These are the grand old Smokey Mountains. Look at them. Ain't they beautiful?"

The tree tops have a bluish-green cast. Fog hovering around the majestic forest gives the mountain range its smoky appearance. "They scare me," I say. "I think I'm a good driver but I wouldn't like to drive up here."

Just then May Lilly wakes up and says she has to go to the bathroom. "Try to hold on, baby until we get out of these mountains. When we come down your uncle can pull into a filling station."

"Look under the seat, Baby Heart. There's a pot in a bag. Let her use that. They may or may not let us use the rest room when we stop at the filling station," Roosevelt says.

"I'm sure they will if you buy gas."

"I've been driving between the North and South more years than you old enough to remember. These crackers don't care if you buy gas or not. That's why I always carry a pot for the ladies. The men can step outside with their backs to the car."

May Lilly doesn't like it but she eases down on the pot and pees. Then she announces that she's hungry. Luckily we have the lunch that she took with her to school this morning.

"That's another thing," Roosevelt says. "Ain't easy to find places that serve colored folks when you traveling in the South. We always pack a lunch. Guess you didn't have time to pack anything today."

"Just May Lilly's lunch for school. Things will be better when we get up North."

"Don't get your hopes up too high. If it's anything like Boston, it's just up South."

"What do you mean by that, Roosevelt?"

"It's segregated but in a different way. They don't have signs out saying White and Colored on the drinking fountains but many of the restaurants don't serve us. Colored people can only live in certain sections of town and can only get low paying hard labor jobs for the most part."

"Then what's the difference? Folks are always coming back home, bragging and acting proud like they're better than us who live down South."

"Like I said Boston is up South and I expect Detroit is no better. Your only hope is to get an education if you want to fare better in the long run. Change is in the air. I don't think colored folks are gonna tolerate being treated this way much longer but the only ones who will be able to make use of opportunities when the doors open will be those with an education."

"Roosevelt, how do you think I'm going to get an education at my age?"

"Age don't have nothing to do with it. I read about a lady eighty years old who just finished high school."

I start thinking maybe Roosevelt is right. Hope springs up in my spirit and I remember my dreams about wearing a nurses cap and white shoes.

DETROIT

1958

Bone tired and sleepy, I see the first sign pointing me to Detroit. We're going through Toledo Ohio and have been on the road over twenty hours, only stopping to go to the bathroom and grab a sandwich after we crossed over the bridge into Cincinnati that divides the South from the North.

I'm driving. Once we leave those Smokey Mountains behind, I tell Roosevelt I can help him drive. He has no trouble turning the wheel over to me. Now he's snoring and May Lilly is fast asleep in the back. I turn on the radio, shut out everything else and listen to the music. Dinah Washington is crooning "What a Difference a Day Makes" in her distinctive soulful voice. I love me some Dinah Washington, especially the way she clearly enunciates every word she sings.

Detroit will be my new home. I wonder what's in store for me in this city I've heard some call the big D. I will make a new start and try to get my children back together. That's all I can think about right now.

At eleven o'clock on Saturday morning I ring the doorbell at 1940 Glendale in Detroit— Candy's address. She opens the door before the echo of the bell fades. I haven't seen her in over six years. Now she stands before me looking no older than she did the last time I saw her. Her sandy hair is styled in a popular short haircut and she looks good.

She flings her arms open and we hug long and hard. "Baby Heart. I'm so glad you made it. I got breakfast waiting."

"I'm so happy to see you, Candy. Do you remember my oldest brother, Roosevelt?"

"Sure. I remember him. And this is May Lilly? She was only a baby last time I saw her. My how she's grown. She's a big girl now."

"May Lilly tell Aunt Candy, hello."

"She's not my auntie. I don't even know her," May Lilly whines.

"Miss Candy's like a sister to me, so you can call her Aunt." May Lilly hides behind me and doesn't say anything.

"That's okay. She'll be in love with me before the end of the week. I teach third grade and have a real way with girls her age. My husband and I don't have any kids yet. We're both excited about having May Lilly and you with us."

"Roosevelt, why don't you bring in the bags? Then we can all sit down and have breakfast. I bet you're hungry." Candy smiles at him.

Roosevelt goes to the car to get our things. Candy and I hold hands and I think about how much I've missed her. Detroit is going to be okay I believe. Except for missing Joel and Cherub, I think Detroit will be a good home for me because Candy is like family.

After breakfast, Candy shows me around her place. It's looks much larger from the outside. I'm surprised that she only has three bedrooms, a dining room, living room, kitchen and one bath. The rooms are spacious and the house is nicely decorated. One of the bedrooms has white furniture. A pink and white canopy covers the top of the bed. The bedspreads and curtains are also pink and white. It's obviously a little girl's room. She squeezes May Lilly's hand and says, "This will be your room, sugar."

May Lilly glances shyly at the big teddy bear sitting on the pink and white pillows and smiles for the first time since we left White Chalk. I let out a sigh of relief. "I can sleep with May Lilly," I tell Candy.

"Oh, no. You will sleep in the guest room."

"I don't want to wear out my welcome. I'll look for my own place as soon as I can. I have some money."

Then Candy explains to me why the house looks so large from the outside. "This is a two family flat," she says. "The upstairs flat is the same as this one. We live downstairs and rent out the upper one. We received notice from the tenants that they're moving next month. You can rent it after they leave if you like it. We will be close together and yet you will have your own space."

"Candy, that will be perfect. I can't believe my good fortune. You're the best friend a girl could ever have. I'm sorry about all of those years that I couldn't talk to you or see you."

"I understand, girl. I'm just happy that you're all right."

"Where is your husband?"

"He had to coach football practice today. Harold's assistant coach at a high school on the east side of Detroit."

"Is he a good husband? Are you happy?"

"Yes. We're perfect for each other. The only thing missing is a baby. We want to start a family soon. You and May Lilly will fill our longing for a family in Detroit. Harold is from Kentucky, so neither of us has family here."

"Having you will help us handle the sadness over the family we had to leave behind. I'm glad we can help each other, Candy."

"The school where I teach is in the district where we live. I can take May Lilly to school with me. What grade is she in?"

"Third."

"Even though I teach third grade, she will be assigned to a different teacher because she lives with me."

We almost forget about Roosevelt who's sitting nodding at the kitchen table. "I'm sorry, Roosevelt. Come on and lie down. You take the guest room tonight," Candy says.

Roosevelt gets up and stretches his big frame, yawns and says, "I wouldn't mind sleeping for a few hours before I hit the road again. I'll leave before midnight, drive all night and make Boston by afternoon Sunday. I have to be at work early Monday morning."

I leave May Lilly watching cartoons on the TV and follow Roosevelt to the guest bedroom where he left my luggage. I open the bag that I put the money in and take out the bundles of cash. "I want you to help me count this," I tell Roosevelt.

"Okay."

I lay five bundles in front of him on the bed and take five. Most of the money is in one hundred dollar bills making it easy to count. Still it takes about half hour to make sure we got it right. After a double count, we're sure of the amount —$20,000.

"That's a lot of cash, Baby Heart. What you gonna to do with it?"

"I'm going to give you some and put the rest in the bank to live off until I can get a job."

"I don't want a penny. Helping you get here is the least I could do after all you've been through. Lincoln and I figured out why you married that scoundrel. We know you did it for the family, to try to save Mama Lilly. We owe you, Baby Heart." He has tears in his eyes.

I don't deny what he just said. "But Roosevelt, I want to at least pay for the gas."

He places a big index finger on my lips and says, "Hush, not another word about giving me money. I want you to think over what I said about going back to school and getting an education. You have enough money there to last about five years if you take care of it and don't throw it away on foolishness."

"I'm gonna pay Candy rent, pay for our food and utilities. I'll need furniture and maybe a car. I'm not gonna throw away any money, you can be sure of that."

"Go to night school. Finish high school at least. Try to go on to college if you can. The more education you get the easier the kind of work you can do. And you'll make more money and get benefits like health insurance."

"Thanks for the advice, Roosevelt. I'll look into school."

"Now the next thing you need to know about is the bank. When you go to open a bank account, don't lug all that money in there and lay it on the counter. They'll want to know where a young colored woman got so much cash. They may report you to the cops or the Internal Revenue for sure."

I'm alarmed. I hadn't thought about having to account for how I came by the money. If I tell them the truth they may contact John El and tell him where I am. Maybe they'll put us all in jail for stealing his money.

"What should I do? Hide it under the mattress?"

"No. Here's what I want you to do. Go to the bank Monday and open a savings account for five hundred dollars. Open a checking account and deposit about two hundred dollars in it for paying your bills. After your accounts are opened, tell them you want to rent a safety deposit box."

"Roosevelt, I don't even know how to write a check. John El never let me take care of any business."

"Candy can show you how. She's a teacher and she looks pretty smart to me. Put the rest of the money in the safety deposit box. When your checking account gets low, take out only what you need from the safety deposit box and put it in the checking account. Add a little at a time to the savings account so you can earn some interest."

"Won't they ask about all the money I'm hiding in the safety deposit box?"

"No. They're not allowed to look at what you're putting in there. You'll be taken into a room that locks behind you. You'll get a key to your box. Lock it and hand it back to the bank clerk when you're through. Then it's locked away in a vault until you need to get into it again. People put all of sorts of things in a safety deposit box—jewelry, important papers, all sorts of valuable stuff. They don't know that it's money you're putting in."

Someone knocks on the door. It's May Lilly. "Mama, I'm hungry."

I lock the suitcase with the money and stick it under the bed. "May Lilly, come on in and tell Uncle Roosevelt good-bye. He's going to sleep and he'll be gone when you wake up in the morning."

She gives him a hug. Roosevelt holds her tight for a minute and then says, "May Lilly, go on back to the kitchen. Your mama will be there in a minute."

After she leaves, closing the door behind her, Roosevelt pulls out a small pearl handled pistol and places it in my hand. "I want you to keep this with you day and night."

He opens the chamber, removes the bullets, and shows me how to aim and fire and how to reload it. "Keep it where May Lilly won't touch it. Make sure she knows it's not a toy. But if John El shows up, I don't want you to be without protection," he says soberly.

The pistol makes me a little squeamish, but I thank him and lock it away with the money before I go to make lunch.

I know May Lilly's missing her big brother and daddy. Harold, Candy's husband comes in while we're having lunch. He's friendly and seems happy to have us. I wouldn't want to feel that we're causing Candy trouble with her husband. So I'm glad he's an easy going, laid back kind of guy.

On Monday morning May Lilly and I leave with Candy so I can enroll her in school. She's whiny and slow. I know she's afraid of a new school and teachers. Everything will be so different than the little country school she's used to with one room and one teacher.

I try to reassure her. "It's gonna be all right, baby. Maybe they will let me stay awhile with you. Would you like that?"

"Yes Ma'am. I won't know nobody there. They may not like me."

"You won't know anybody there." I correct her. "You're such a sweet, smart girl they're bound to like you as soon as they get to know you."

I think back to my first day at Marysville High when the other girl's ganged up on Candy and me because we were new. I know it's not going to be easy for her. I hug her close to me. She's dressed in a pretty dress and I make sure her hair part is straight and her braids have pretty ribbons tied to the ends. "Aunt Candy will be there too. She won't be in the same room but she'll be in the same building."

The school is real big. I had no idea an elementary school would be so large. I wonder how she'll find her way to class without help. I get her enrolled and ask the teacher if I can stay for a while. She says if I insist but she thinks May Lillie will adjust faster if I leave. I look back as I walk to the door and wave to her. Her face is clouded, like she thinks I lied to her. I hate to leave her but I have to trust the teacher on this.

I catch the bus to head back home following the route Candy told me to take. I board the bus, feeling uncertain. I drop my coins in the slot, get a transfer and ask the driver if he will call the stop where I transfer to the next bus. I'm still standing not knowing to hold on to the pole when he lurches off. I lose my balance and almost falls. He yells, "Hold on to the pole lady or sit down."

I'm afraid to try to find a seat, so I hold on tight until he gets to the next stop. I hold my heart and look for a seat while more passengers crowd onto the bus. When he calls my stop, I'm afraid to stand up with the bus still moving and I don't know I have to pull the cord. So he keeps going. At the next stop someone else pulls the cord. I hang on to the seats as I sway my way to the door; afraid I'm going to fall.

I throw away the transfer and walk the rest of the way home following the route Candy drove to get to the school. I'm exhausted when I reach Glendale. I notice the morning paper rolled up on the porch and take it inside with me. After my experience on the DSR bus I know the first thing I have to do is buy a car.

I spend most of the morning going through the classified section for cars. There are pages and pages of autos for sale. I think about buying a new car. I can easily pay the two thousand or more that's advertised for a new Chevrolet. I remember what Roosevelt said about spending my money wisely and decide that I better select a used one. I may need money for more important things like a hospital bill.

When Candy and May Lilly come home from school, May Lilly is all smiles. She likes her new school and her teacher. She even made a friend or two. This eases my mind.

I tell Candy about my bus ride. "I'm scared to death that bullet will move into my heart if I get on another bus. I read through the ads in the paper and saw a lot of cars that I can afford. Would you and Harold go with me Saturday to look for a car?"

"Why wait until Saturday? We can take you this evening."

We pile into the car with Harold and Candy to go shopping. Harold drives over to Livernois Avenue, not very far from where we live. He says, "Livernois is lined with used car lots. You're sure to find something you like here. The trick will be getting credit when you're new in town and not working yet."

I tell him, "I brought a thousand dollars with me. I looked in the paper and I'm sure I can get a used car I want for under a thousand."

He looks at me raises his eyebrows. "You mean to tell me you got a thousand dollars in your pocket book? I have to work three months for that kind of money."

"Yeah. I have a little money but I have to be careful how I spend it. It has to last me for five years."

We look at several lots. Some of the salesmen are too busy to help us. Harold says the all white sales staff just doesn't want to be bothered with colored folks.

I wonder if they know our money is green just like white folks. When we get to the third lot, I find a blue and beige 1955 Chevrolet Impala. It looks clean and there are no dents on it. The price on the windshield of $750.00 fits my budget nicely. I tell Harold "We have to talk to a salesman. This is just what I want. Maybe they will let you test drive it."

Harold goes inside and comes back with a half-hearted salesman. "I hear you're interested in this car. I'll need your credit information and a deposit before I can let you or your friend test drive it."

"I wasn't planning to apply for credit."

He smirks, "How you think you're going to pay for it?"

"Cash."

"You mean to tell me you got $750.00 plus taxes and cost of license plates in cash."

"Yes Sir."

He turns all red in the face and says "Come on inside. I need to see it."

We follow him to his desk where I go through the humiliation of counting out my money. This is worse than down South I think. I haven't gone through something like this since John El bought my wedding rings. When he walks into stores in Marysville or Atlanta white folks are all over him, eager to wait on him. They know he pays for everything cash and they don't give him any hassle. I remember what Roosevelt told me about Detroit and Boston and probably all the other big cities in the North.

The salesman says to me, "Leave the money here if you want to test-drive the car."

I look him square in the eyes and say, "I will leave a deposit of ten percent or $75.00. If we don't like the car, you will give me my deposit back. Otherwise, I'll take my business elsewhere." I get up from his desk, toss my hair and motion the others to follow.

He smiles and hands me the keys.

I count out seventy-five dollars and wait for a written receipt saying that the money will be refunded if the car is returned in the same condition it was in. If I decide to buy the car the deposit will be subtracted from the purchase price.

As we walk out the door, Harold seems surprised. "I like the way you spoke up to him. Most women wouldn't have had the nerve."

Candy laughs and says, "You haven't seen nothing yet. Jolee Baby Heart Turner Murphy is tougher than steel, able to repel flying bullets and live with the devil himself. Putting a white man in his place is one of the easiest things she can do."

I would have been offended if anyone else had said that. But coming from Candy it was a compliment. I smile all the way back to Glendale in my new blue Impala.

I get directions from Candy and Harold to the bank and the Adult Education program she told me about. When they leave for school next day, I head for the bank. After the bank I'm off to enroll in school.

Adult day school is nothing like regular high school. Classes are held in one room in an old dreary gray building. There are two teachers to help about forty-five students ranging from teenage high school dropouts to senior citizens. The few white students are immigrants who don't speak English well. I feel sorry for them trying to earn a high school diploma and learn English at the same time. We're not there to socialize or make friends. We are on different levels and allowed to study and learn at our own pace with individual help from the teachers.

I receive a workbook on the ninth grade level. I'm allowed to take it home with me after I pay for it. I'm eager to study and supplement my learning with outside books. I know I can depend on help from Candy. I hold that workbook close to me like it's pure gold and can't wait to get home and start learning.

 33

ON MY OWN

After Candy's tenants leave, May Lilly and I move upstairs.

Picking out my own furniture is exciting. I never got to choose anything in our house in White Chalk. Everything was already there. If anything needed replacing, John El did the choosing.

For my flat, I buy all modern furniture. Blond is in style, so I get blond coffee table and end tables, a brown and beige couch with blond wood trim and matching lamps for the end tables. I buy two bedroom suites; twin beds for May Lilly, blond of course and gray lacquer finish for my bedroom. I decide not to buy dining room furniture. I need to save my money and use the space as a study room. So I buy three folding card tables and six folding chairs. A bookcase provides a place to store and organize our books. If we ever have more company than we can fit around the yellow Formica, chrome trimmed kitchen table,

I'll push the three card tables together and cover them with a pretty tablecloth.

Due to my thrifty shopping, I'm able to furnish the flat for a little over six hundred dollars.

Candy says, "Baby Heart, you got it looking good up here. I can't believe you bought all this stuff for what you spent."

I feel proud of myself. "Yeah, I'm learning to stretch a buck. Being an unemployed single mother with a health problem, I've got to be careful how I spend my money."

After school on weekdays, May Lilly and I sit in our study room, doing homework together. I don't date. Harold tried to fix me up with a single buddy of his. I went with him to a drive-in movie one Saturday. I couldn't keep my mind on him or the picture, though he seemed nice enough. Rather than waste any man's time and money, I don't accept dates. My heart and spirit are too wounded.

Joel and Cherub fill my thoughts in the daytime and dreams at night. I would give anything to hear their voices and hold them close to me. I write a letter to each of them every week. Then I call Roosevelt to see if he received the letters and mailed them on. Our conversation always goes the same:

"Roosevelt, did you get the letters I mailed a few days ago?"

"Yeah. I got them Baby Heart, and mailed them on."

"Did I receive mail from the kids?"

"Afraid not. If I get any, I'll forward it to you the same day."

When Christmas shopping starts right after Thanksgiving, I write them both asking what they want for Christmas but they don't answer. I think John El isn't giving my letters to Joel and maybe Willie Lee is withholding Cherub's but I keep on writing.

Christmas shopping lifts my spirits. I splurge on gifts for all three of my children. I get presents for Papa Joe, too. I send the presents to Georgia via Boston through Roosevelt. He lets me know he got them and sent them on. But he adds, "I think you're wastin' your money. You'll never know if they get the gifts."

"Maybe not, Roosevelt. But I couldn't live with myself if I didn't try. I miss them so much until I think about going back down there to try and steal them away."

"Don't do it. Talk to Lincoln. He can visit the kids for you and let you know how they're doin'."

"I talk to him about once a week. He went to see them Thanksgiving and took Papa Joe with him. He said they were fine. He didn't ask if they had heard from me because John El and Willie Lee never left them alone with the kids."

"There, I told you they're alright. Don't do nothing foolish. When they get older, they'll come to you. Until then you have to be patient."

"I guess you're right. But I sure do miss them. I'm glad I have May Lilly. She caught right on at school. She gets all A grades and she's made friends, too."

"I'm not surprised. She's smart like her mama. You hold on. Maybe Linc can drive up this summer and bring Papa Joe and the kids to see you."

"I don't think their fathers will let them come. But you know it's a funny thing. Linc said he was ready for a confrontation with John El when he went to White Chalk but John El never mentioned May Lilly or me and the missing money. He sat in a corner watching the kids and talked quietly with Papa Joe."

"He's a strange man. I think he knows he did you wrong and was expecting you to leave him. He knew you had that money coming. You didn't clean him out, only took as much as you needed to get by. A man has to respect a woman like that."

"I think Joel is his most prized possession. I have a feeling if I had taken his son he would have moved earth and hell to get him back. I'm still not breathing easy, Roosevelt. I look over my shoulder all the time and up and down the street for his car before I go in the house every day."

"Try not to worry, little sister. I have a feeling that Candy and her husband are gonna look out for y'all."

"Yeah, I know. But Harold isn't like you and Linc. I think he's more the intellectual type. I doubt if he would be a match for John El."

"Are you keeping that pearl handled pistol, I gave you, in your purse when you go out and nearby when you sleep?"

"Yeah, I am. But I still feel unsafe just the same."

I end the phone conversation and look out my window at another gray day. That's the one thing I hate about Detroit — too many drab, gray days. It's hard for me to get my spirits up when I can't see sunshine.

34

ANGELS IN MY LIFE

The snow and ice have melted away and Easter of 1959 is approaching. This isn't my favorite holiday season. Bad things happen to me around Easter time, like bargaining myself off to John El and losing my mother. Then I was shot in the heart last year on the Saturday before Easter. An eerie feeling comes over me like something bad is about to happen again.

Dismiss negative thoughts of gloom and doom I tell myself.

Planning Easter dinner for both our families with Candy lifts my spirits. We'll eat downstairs in her flat. Candy and I decided on the menu and bought all of the food together. We will have ham, potato salad, greens, macaroni and cheese, hot rolls and lemonade. At the last minute late Saturday evening, I get a craving for pickled peaches to serve over the greens.

Mama Lilly knew how to pickle peaches. I never learned. Besides we don't have time for canning. But there's a neighborhood market that carries food favored by Southern-raised folks. I grab my purse and rush out the door hoping to get to the Dexter Market before it closes.

The owner, Mr. Rubenstein is in the store when I get there. He's a short, slightly stooped, older Jewish man with a full head of black hair. I met Morrie Rubenstein not long after I moved to Detroit. He teases me because I go in the store often looking for souse meat which he calls head cheese. For a long time he didn't know what I was talking about.

I speak to him this evening and say, "I won't take long, Mr. Rubenstein. I'm looking for pickled peaches. That's all I need."

"Look in aisle six for canned fruit. You're our last customer. I have to count the day's receipts." He smiles, removes money from the cash register and starts counting. The only employee still there locks the door and turns the sign over to read "closed."

I make my way swiftly through the store to the canned fruit section. My eyes search through rows of fruit cocktail, pears, pineapples, cherries and plain peaches. I'm about to give up when I spot them on a higher shelf. In my haste, I forget I'm not supposed to make sudden moves or reach above my head. I stand on tiptoes, extend my arm to reach as far up as I can and grab the heavy jar of pickled peaches.

Pain grips me and shoots through my chest like a bolt of lighting. I feel the deadly bullet move into my heart as the jar of peaches slips from my hand and crashes onto the floor. Down I sink into the mixture of syrupy peach juice and glass that smells spicy like cloves. A scream escapes my lips as I press my hand to my chest.

Mr. Rubenstein rushes over. "Jolee, what's wrong?"

"Call an ambulance. A bullet's in my heart."

As I drift away, I hear him say in a dumbfounded voice, "What are you talking about? You haven't been shot. There's nobody here but Johnny and me and he's in the back."

Darkness surrounds me as my eyelids slowly descend. I make one last weak plea, "Please call an ambulance."

A sterile antiseptic smell enters my nostrils before my eyes open and I know I'm in a hospital. I just can't remember why. My eyelashes flutter and open slowly. A man is standing on one side of the bed with a stethoscope pressed to my chest. He looks young but judging by the green scrub suit and stethoscope, I think he's a doctor.

A nurse is standing on the other side. I look beyond them to where Candy and Morrie stand looking worried. "Why am I here?" I ask weakly. I can barely hear my own voice.

The doctor speaks. "You're at Detroit Receiving Hospital. I'm Doctor Muskat. You were brought in by ambulance because you collapsed. Your friend has given us some history. She says you have a bullet lodged in or near your heart."

"It moved. The doctors at Grady Hospital in Atlanta told me that the bullet was lodged partly in my heart muscle. They said it was too dangerous to operate. Just before I blacked out I felt it move. I believe it's all the way in my heart." I begin to cry, thinking I should be dead. Maybe I would be better off dead than live in fear.

"Calm down," Doctor Muskat says. "Actually you may be better off with the bullet fully embedded in the heart if you have no symptoms or complications."

I look at him and wonder how he can be so calm. "Doctor, I can't go on like this. I mean living in fear that if I make one false move or if a complication sets in, I may die. Can't you operate and get this thing out of me?"

"First we will have to perform a transeophageal echocardiogram to determine the exact location of the bullet. This is a trauma hospital. Doctors here are skilled in emergency care. If the position of the projectile is found to be life threatening, surgery may be indicated."

Morrie Rubenstein steps forward. "Didn't you hear the young lady, Doctor? She wants the bullet removed. As long as that bullet is inside her, she feels her life is threatened."

Doctor Muskat looks at Morrie as though he just realized that he was standing there. "Who are you?" he asks.

"I'm Morrie Rubenstein. Jolee was in my market when she collapsed. I rode with her in the ambulance to the hospital."

The doctor frowns, "Only close relatives are allowed in the examining room. I'm afraid you have to leave or wait in the emergency waiting area."

"She's my daughter," Morrie says without blinking.

The doctor looks at me and back at Morrie suspiciously. "Is this man your father?"

"My adoptive father," I answer.

"Still, you both have to realize it's not her option entirely. Surgery to remove projectiles lodged in or near the heart is being performed more often with a high degree of success but there is still great risk with any heart surgery. If the bullet is fully imbedded and the patient is asymptomatic, the operation would be elective. In that case the hospital or insurance, if she has insurance, will not accept the cost."

"If it's about money, don't worry. I will pay." Morrie says.

"Do you have any idea how much the surgery alone will cost?" the doctor asks Morrie.

"Yes, I do. My daughter's life is my concern. Go ahead with the test and let us know the results. But if she decides to take the risk regardless of the outcome, money is no object."

"I want to speak with my father privately," I whisper.

"We need to get you into the exam room as quickly as possible. But go ahead and take a minute to talk things over with your dad," Dr. Muskat says.

Candy and the nurse leave first followed by the doctor who pulls the white curtain closed behind him.

Morrie comes over and takes my hand in his.

"Mr. Rubenstein, I don't understand why you're offering to do this. I barely know you and I'm certainly not your daughter. I can't allow a strange man to pay my medical bill. I'm afraid of what I may owe you. That's how I got to where I am now, owing a man for a hospital bill."

Morrie holds onto my hand. His eyes are moist, "My child, I have no sexual motives. I'm an old man with a wife I dearly love. I've watched you ever since you started coming into my store; watched the way you carry yourself, how loving you seem with your little girl. Then when your friend Candy told me what you've been through, I decided I want to help. I have plenty money but I have never had children. Let me help you. All I ask in return is that you treat me like a father."

"I appreciate all that you've done but I have to be careful about accepting help. Anyhow, I have a father. His name is Joe Turner. I call him Papa Joe. He's a poor man but he's a good father. No one can take his place." I see the doctor coming back in the room.

An orderly wheels me away to another room where I will undergo a procedure to determine exactly where the deadly souvenir from John El is located. I lie on my left side like the doctor instructed and close my eyes. I don't want to think anymore. I'm tired of worry and fear, which have been my constant companions for so long. I need to rest.

Examinations finished, I'm returned to the large room divided by white curtains with rows of patients behind them. I quickly learn that Saturday nights in a big city emergency room of a trauma hospital is what a visit to hell must be like.

From bits and pieces of conversation that float over my curtain and the sight of bandaged heads and chests, I find out that some patients have entered the hospital with fresh gunshot or stab wounds. Others have suffered heart attacks or survived automobile crashes. Doctors and nurses rush frantically around looking over test results and talking to each other after they have stabilized the patients who lie groaning or screaming in pain.

In spite of all of the hard work and responsibility the medical staff has, I wish I were in their shoes instead of lying helplessly on this gurney waiting to know my fate. It seems my role in life is patient instead of nurse, which is what I hoped to be.

Candy pulls the curtain and comes in followed by Morrie.

"Y'all still here?" I ask.

"You didn't think we would leave you alone, did you?" Candy answers.

I know Candy wouldn't leave me but I still can't understand why Morrie Rubenstein is sticking around. Dr. Muskat comes in. The expression on his face is serious. I sense bad news coming.

The doctor clears his throat, pulls a stool close to the head of my stretcher, sits down and says, "It seems like you're going to get your wish, Mrs. Murphy. The examination has revealed cardiac arrhythmia which is life threatening. I recommend surgery. However, you should know that the survival rate is only fifty percent."

"Doctor, I'll take the risk. I'm hanging my hopes on the fifty percent chance the operation will be a success and give me a normal life."

"Should I make arrangements for payment in the business office?" Morrie asks.

"Since her condition is classified as an emergency, the hospital will absorb the loss unless she has resources. She is an adult. You are not required to pay the bill, Mr. Rubenstein."

Morrie puffs out his chest proudly and says, "My daughter doesn't accept charity, Doctor. I will handle it." He leaves the room, heading for the business office I suppose, before I can say a word.

"When will the operation take place, Doctor?" I ask.

"Tonight. It's an emergency. Our odds for success may be less the longer we delay."

"I'm ready. I would like a minute alone with my friend before they take me to the operating room."

The doctor goes out and pulls the curtain, leaving Candy and me alone. "Candy, come closer."

She walks over and holds my hand, looking at me with the old look in her eyes I remember from childhood. The one that says without speaking, 'I'm here for you girlfriend.'

"What do you make of Mr. Rubenstein, Candy? I've told him I don't want to be obligated to him."

"He seems sincere to me. Sometimes God puts angels in our lives. Maybe Mr. Rubenstein is your guardian angel. Don't turn him away."

"You are my witness. I didn't ask for his help. I don't owe him."

Candy caresses my forehead. "We know, Baby Heart. You don't owe him anything."

"Candy, promise me if I don't make it that you'll raise May Lilly. I don't want John El to get her."

"I love May Lilly like she's my own daughter. I promise to do everything in my power to keep her if she needs a mother. But I don't think I'll have to raise your daughter. You're going to make it, Baby Heart. Morrie and I will be here waiting for you when you come down from the operating room."

"You should go home. The surgery might take a long time. All night, even."

"Then we'll see you in the morning or tomorrow afternoon. However long it takes, we'll be here waiting."

"Who's gonna take care of May Lilly?"

"Harold is home with her. I called just before you came back down. She's fine."

"And Mr. Rubenstein. Shouldn't he be taking care of his business or go home to his wife?"

"Mr. Rubenstein has made arrangements. Don't worry about a thing. Focus all of your energy on getting that bullet out of your heart so you can get well."

"I will," I promise as they wheel me away to the operating room. On the way, I remember what Candy said about God putting angels in my life. I know she's one of my angels. I still wonder about Morrie Rubenstein.

I'm slid carefully from the gurney onto the operating table. A team of doctors and nurses line each side of the table with surgical masks covering their faces. I recognize Doctor Muskat behind his mask and wave bravely at him.

"You okay, Mrs.Murphy?" he asks.

"Yes, Doctor," I feel a shot in my arm. A mask is placed over my face. I drift into peaceful twilight and then slumber.

Sterile whiteness is all I see at first.

The doctors have disappeared. One nurse sits by my side intently watching a machine that is making soft beeping noises. I look closely at the machine and see a needle moving across a screen in peaks and valleys.

I'm impatient to get this operation over with before I lose my nerve. "Nurse, where did the doctors go? Why haven't they operated on me yet?"

"My dear, you're in the recovery room. The operation was successfully completed several hours ago. Welcome back. I have been monitoring your progress. I'm happy to tell you, you're doing fine, came through the operation like a champ."

I can't believe I have gone through hours of surgery and have spent several more hours sleeping in the recovery room. It seems to me no time has elapsed since the doctor stuck a needle in my arm. Maybe this is the way it will be when we die. We will wake up on judgment morning thousands of years later, but it will be like the blink of an eye, like no time has passed at all.

"Nurse, did they take the bullet out?"

"Yes they did. Want to see it?"

"I need to think about that. Maybe I do. Maybe I don't."

"Your family members have waited all night to see you. Do you feel well enough for visitors?"

"Yes Ma'am. Please send for them to come in." I feel my arms and pinch myself. The quick, tiny pain from the pinch feels good. I'm alive. I no longer have a bullet in my heart. I feel joy move into the space the bullet once occupied and spread through my whole body, filling it to the brim. It overflows into my spirit and lifts me up.

Thank you God for my life and the angels that surround me, including the doctors, nurses, Candy and Morrie Rubenstein, I pray.

GETTING TO KNOW MORRIE

I remain in the hospital for two weeks following my surgery. Candy comes to see me every day. They won't let May Lilly visit. No children under age twelve are allowed. Candy brings notes from her, telling me how much she loves and misses me. She says she'll be glad when I come home but not to worry because Aunt Candy and Uncle Harold are taking good care of her. Her letters cheer me. I feel strength returning to my body, the kind of robust energy I had before John El shot me.

Morrie has visited often since the operation. I'm getting to know him better. On the day of my scheduled discharge, a doctor comes to my room early. He hands me papers and say I will recuperate slowly and need four more weeks of bed rest before I resume normal duties.

"I don't know how I can stay in bed" I tell the doctor. "The only family I have here is my eight year old daughter. She has to go to school. My best friend lives downstairs but she works as a teacher. She's been so kind to me already. I can't burden her with my care."

"I'll have one of our hospital social workers meet with you before you leave. She may be able to help you with community resources like the visiting health nurse and home care help," the doctor says

I thank him and wait for the social worker who never comes. Late that afternoon, I see Candy stroll into the room. She's pretty as a Georgia peach in a yellow linen two- piece dress. Her smile fills the hospital room like rays of sunshine.

She squeezes my hand. "Baby Heart, I see you're dressed and ready to go. May Lilly is waiting downstairs with Harold. We're so glad you're coming home."

My mood doesn't match Candy's. I'm worried about being confined to bed for another month.

"What am I going to do now?" I ask Candy. "The doctor says I'll need another four weeks of bed rest. Can you take me to the social work department before we leave? The doctor said they might be able to arrange help at home. I can't burden you with my care."

"Don't worry about a thing. Morrie and I have made arrangements for all the help you will need. All you have to do is get well. I need some help though. Getting all these flowers and fruit baskets, that Morrie sent you, home isn't going to be easy."

I shake my head and look at Candy "I'm getting more and more into Morrie's debt. I'm afraid, Candy. He must be up to something."

The weeks pass swiftly. Bed rest isn't as bad as I had expected. Candy brings me homework from my school. I'm able to walk slowly into the study and work at the table for an hour or two during the day. A visiting nurse comes twice a week and checks my vital signs, changes the bandages and tells me I'm progressing fine.

Then there's Kate, a heavyset woman who Morrie hired to cook and wait on me hand and foot. And Morrie comes every Monday loaded with books and gifts that I try to refuse. I learn a lot more about him. In addition to the market, he owns two nightclubs. He calls them black and tan clubs because they cater to whites and Negroes, which is unusual in Detroit.

"I'm a businessman, Jolee. But I always wanted to be a musician. I love jazz. Owning nightclubs allow me to listen to the best music and get to know famous entertainers. I love it," he tells me one Monday over lunch of chicken salad and iced tea.

I change the subject. "Morrie, I still don't understand why you're doing so much for me." A frown creases my forehead as I wait for his response.

Morrie looks at me with a wizened smile. "Do people need a motive to be nice?"

"You must admit it's very unusual for a man to help a woman he's not related to without expecting something in return."

"I told you what I expect. I want you to be my daughter."

"Don't you think we make a strange father-daughter pair? I mean a Jewish man and a colored girl?"

"Not at all. You're thinking the way prejudiced, racists have programmed you to think. I chose you for my daughter. Therefore you are. No one else has a damned thing to do with it. Just you and me and Esther of course."

"Who is Esther?

"My wife. She always wanted a daughter. As soon as you're well enough, I want to take you to meet her."

"What if she doesn't like me?"

"Esther is one of the most loving humans on earth. She'll love you. I always wanted to grant her every desire. A child is the only thing I haven't been able to give her. She had a hard life. Born in Germany. She survived the Holocaust. I met her after the war ended. She had found safety with relatives here in Detroit.

"We fell in love and were married. I had been married before. My first wife died childless when we both were in our forties. When Esther and I got together, it was too late for us to have children. But I know she feels she missed out on a big part of life —getting to be a mother and having grandchildren. I want to give her that before she dies."

"Morrie, is she okay? I mean the way you said 'before she dies.'"

His eyes moisten. He unfolds his napkin and wipes them. "Esther doesn't have long to live. Will you help me give her the daughter and grandchild she never had?"

Now I understand Morrie. There's room in my heart for another father and a mother, too. "Sure, Morrie. As soon as I'm able to get about, the first thing I want to do is meet Miz Esther."

"After you get to know her, maybe you can call her Mother. And May Lilly might call her Bubbe. She'd like that."

"Bubbe? What does that mean?"

"Oh, it's just another name for grandmother that Jewish kids use."

Esther Rubenstein is something else.

On the first Sunday that I'm able to go out, Morrie comes for May Lilly and me. I'm nervous. May Lilly knows she's going to meet Mrs. Rubenstein who may become her Grandma. She has never known a grandmother. So she's excited. But I keep thinking what if Miz Esther doesn't like us.

I whisper to Morrie, "You told her that we're coming?"

He takes my hand in his, smiles and says reassuringly, "Certainly."

"Does she know?"

"Know what?"

"That we're colored."

"There was no need to tell her. She couldn't care less about what color or race people are."

We walk with Morrie into her bedroom. She's propped up in bed, with her long white hair fanned out over the pillows. Her face still retains a beauty that shows no ravages of suffering or aging. Radiance sparkles from her eyes when she sees us and fills the room with warmth and love.

A scent like mixed perfume fragrances drifts through her bedroom reminding me of Hudson's Department Store, where I went shopping once with Candy. I had never smelled anything like the first floor of Hudson's. The perfume counters are near the entrance. I am told that the salesladies spray a mixture of perfumes every morning to give off the fragrance that Hudson's is known for. I had expected a sick room odor, but Miss Esther's room smells sweet, like Hudson's Department store.

She lays a book aside and extends both hands when she sees us enter the room. "My children. Come."

I walk over to the bed. She takes my brown hands in her frail white ones. She looks at me a long time before she says, "My daughter. I've waited for you so long. You are beautiful."

Awkwardness overcomes me. Being expected to think of a woman I just met as my mother is a strange feeling, especially since I'm a grown woman who knew and loved my mother. This woman has love shining from her eyes. Though her hands are cold, I know her heart is warm. I don't want to give in to the emotion swelling in me. If I accept and return her love, I'll have to bear the pain of losing her. I've been through enough loss and grief. I don't want it again. I turn away and call to May Lilly, "Come meet Mrs. Rubenstein."

I see the pain of rejection flash through Esther Rubenstein's eyes. I correct myself, "Come closer, May Lilly and give Grandmother Esther a hug."

May Lilly puts her arms around Esther and says "Hello, Bubbe," her voice sweet with innocence.

Soon we are sitting around Mother Esther's bed in plush blue velvet chairs, talking to her like we've known her all of our lives. I feel comfortable with this beautiful lady who smiles through her pain and wants to know all about us.

After our initial meeting, Morrie arranges for us to spend weekends in Oak Park with him and Mother Esther. I read to her, comb her hair, make up her face but mostly we talk like mother and daughter. I tell her my life stories and she tells me hers. We both have horror stories. Perhaps we should leave them buried in the past. But as we talk, we grow closer. Sharing dreadful memories make them less painful.

Morrie wants to pay me for the weekend companionship. I remind him if we're going to be a real family, a daughter shouldn't be paid for visiting her parents. He agrees. But a funny thing happens. When I try to pay my bills, they have already been paid.

One day he gives me keys to a new car —a Cadillac. I say firmly, "Morrie, I really can't accept this. You've gone too far."

"You must have reliable transportation. I will not have my grandchild in a car that might break down in traffic. Besides what if we need you and your car won't start?"

"Okay, Morrie. It's useless to argue with you." I accept the car keys and the new yellow Cadillac. The joy in their eyes is undeniable when they give us presents.

Then one day, about three months after we met her, while I'm reading to Mother Esther her eyes close. I think she has drifted off to sleep and get up to leave the room.

She screams, "Come back. Don't leave me. I'll stay with you. Come back to me."

At first, I think she's talking to me. But she calls their names, her mother, father, brother and sisters. I realize she's talking to her family who was killed in German death camps.

Non-Jewish friends smuggled Esther into Austria where she was safe. She told me that she still feels guilty that her family perished while she survived.

I put my arms around her and soothe her like she's a baby. "Hush, Mother Esther. You couldn't save them. They wanted you to live. That way a part of them lived on."

Her eyes are still closed. She whispers, "You came. You have come back for me. Don't you see them, Jolee? They're here, all around my bed."

I lean over the bed and gently rock her in my arms.

A beautiful smile spreads across her face. "Goodbye, Daughter. Tell Morrie and May Lilly I love them but I must go home with my other family now."

I stroke her hair. She shudders. One soft whoosh of air escapes from her slightly parted thin lips and she's gone.

36

FREE AT LAST

A healthy life in the big city, without a husband to answer to, gives me understanding of the meaning of freedom.

I don't have to ask permission to go out or invite my family for a visit. So I do both.

I call Lincoln and ask him to come up on his summer vacation and bring Papa Joe with him and Joel and Cherub, too if he can.

He says he and Papa Joe will come for sure. He doesn't think he'll be able to bring the children. "Even if John El and Willie Lee would let them come, I don't think it's a good idea. They might go back and tell him where you are. You been through too much to have that fool track you down and hurt you all over again."

I settle for a visit from Papa Joe and Lincoln. While I'm looking forward to their visit, I accept an invitation from Morrie to come to his Flamingo Club one Saturday night. Candy and Harold come with me. I've never been to a nightclub before. I wear my hair in a sophisticated French Twist. My black off the shoulder cocktail dress is formfitting and shows off all of my assets in a classy way.

A long line has formed that's winding around the block when we arrive. Morrie told me what to do, so we walk to the front of the line where the doorman is beginning to let people in for the second show. The doorman looks at us and says, "The line starts around the corner."

I clear my throat, and say, "I'm Morrie Rubenstein's daughter. And these are my friends." I point to Harold and Candy.

The doorman doesn't try to conceal his curiosity, but he says politely, "Follow me."

Morrie sees us come in and drops what he's doing to personally escort us to the best seats in the club. Heads turn and I hear whispers, "Is she a singer or one of the exotic dancers?"

The Flamingo Cub is magnificent. Crystal chandeliers give off a low mellow glow. Beautiful women and men, sit around tables decorated in colors of peach and black. White, black, brown and yellow people mix while they wait for the show to begin. It's a different world to me, where race and color don't seem to matter. All the people are there for the same thing — to be entertained.

A dancer opens the show. She's introduced as Dottie the body. They call her an exotic dancer but Harold whispers to me that she's really a strip teaser or shake dancer.

Dottie takes the stage dressed like a queen in a flowing purple evening gown with a tiara on her head. She dances gracefully around the stage at first. Then she goes into rhythmic bumps and grinds, slowly stripping off everything except a tassel over each tit and a string between her legs. Before the act ends, Dottie is doing push-ups. Acting like a man's underneath her and she's screwing him into the floor, while still keeping time to the music.

I'm embarrassed. I've never seen anything like this before. I can't help wondering what John El would do if he knew I was in a place like this.

Seeing Morrie in the nightclub gives me a different image of him. I watch him out of the corner of my eye and know that he's enjoying the act. He holds his shoulders erect and a manliness that I've never noticed before creeps over him. Morrie is still interested in women, I realize.

I nurse a drink and watch the show.

The main attraction takes center stage. He's Stan Crooke, a famous rhythm and blues singer. Candy has all of his records. He's our favorite recording artist. Stan is handsome— a deep chocolate brown with dreamy eyes and a build like Bobby Joe. His appearance and the sweet love songs he croons, bring back memories. I wipe a tear from my eye.

"What's wrong, Baby Heart?" Candy asks.

"Nothing. He reminds me of someone. That's all."

"He sure does. Looks a lot like Bobby Joe Miller. I wonder what happened to him."

"I don't know but I sure would like to find out."

"I'll call Cousin Trudy. Maybe she knows where he is."

At the end of the second show, Stan Crooke comes over to our table and sits down. He beckons the waitress over and orders drinks for all of us.

"You all know who I am. I hear you're Morrie's daughter," he says looking me over with eyes hot as burning coals.

I nod. "My name is Jolee Murphy. These are my friends, Candy and Harold. Thanks for the drinks."

A comedian is letting go with a barrage of raunchy jokes warming up for the third and final act.

Before Stan Crooke has to go back on stage, he says, "I'll be appearing here for another week. May I have your phone number? I would like to see more of you before I leave."

I haven't been around much. But I know from what I've read about him that he's married and likes to play. I smile politely and say, "Thanks, but I can't go out with you."

"Are you really Morrie Rubenstein's daughter or is he your sugar daddy?" he asks loud enough for everyone to hear.

"Morrie is my father. I can't go out with you because I'm married. And if I wasn't I still wouldn't go out with you because you're rude."

He mutters, "Sorry I wasted my time," as he heads back on stage to lull the audience into a world of romantic fantasy with his sweet love songs.

"What a jerk," Harold says. "Guess you and Candy won't be swooning over his records anymore."

Candy keeps her promise. The next day she calls Miz Trudy Miller. We both talk to her. It's good to hear from her again but she doesn't know where Bobby Joe is living. Says she saw him when he came home for his mother's funeral several years ago. He stayed overseas after he was discharged from the service. She thinks he married a woman over there. She doesn't recall if he said which country he's living in.

I tuck my daydreams away and get on with my life. A life that will never include the man I love and I'm not ready to settle for a substitute.

 *37*

SUMMER 1960

Days turn swiftly into weeks, weeks into months and soon I've been living in Detroit for two years.

Today is my last day of school. By studying hard and with help from Candy, I've received my high school diploma in less than two years.

Thunder rumbles in the distance as I leave school. I sniff the air and smell rain. A summer storm is making up. I hurry to the parking lot with my mind on the future when I recall a conversation that I had recently with Morrie. I told him I wanted to take a nine-month course to become a Licensed Practical Nurse.

He looked at me with disappointment and said, "Never half-step, Jolee. If you want to become a nurse, go to college and get a full degree so you will have the credentials for a registered nurse."

"But, Morrie," I had said. "I'm almost twenty-eight years old and have a child to support. I need to get to work. You've done so much for me already. I don't expect you to take care of us for four years while I go to college."

"I want my daughter to become the best that she can be. If I don't spend my money on you and May Lilly, what am I supposed to do with it? I'm an old man. I don't have anybody else."

I gave in and promised Morrie I would go to college. I applied to Marygrove and Wayne State University. I don't know yet if I will be accepted.

As I drive home many thoughts run through my mind. What's it like to be a college student? Can I do the work? Doubt and fear nag at me. Jazz is playing on the car radio. I relax and thoughts of celebration leap joyfully into my head. I'll have a small dinner party where Candy, Harold, Morrie, May Lilly and I can celebrate my high school graduation.

Rain drops form on the windshield as I near the street where I live. Lightning flashes across the dark sky followed by a loud clap of thunder and a downpour of rain. Luckily the parking space in front of my house is vacant. I scramble out of the car and run up the steps to my flat. My key turns easily in the lock.

The door opens and joy turns to fear as I look into the cold, green eyes of the devil.

He sits facing the door with Cherub on his lap. May Lilly is standing behind him with her arms around his neck. My mouth opens and closes without a sound. My instinct is to turn and run. But I can't leave my children.

His eyes bore through me. Then he says as calm as you please, "Baby Heart, ain't you happy to see yo' husban' and niece?"

I stare at Cherub. She's fourteen now, the same age I was when he made up his mind that I was gonna be his wife. She looks older than fourteen. Her breasts are large and pointed. Sandy hair frames her heart-shaped face in silky ringlets; same as when she was a baby. She makes no effort to come to me. She doesn't even speak.

"What's going on?" I ask finally. "Why are ya'll here?"

"You mean we're not welcome," he says through a sneer.

"I'm glad to see you, Cherub. Come give your Aunt Baby Heart a hug."

She gets up, walks over to where I'm still standing just inside the door. " Hey, Ant Baby heart." She gives me a little peck on the cheek and goes back to him and plops down on his lap.

I could be risking another bullet but I have to ask, "How did you find us, John El?"

"May Lilly sent me a Father's Day card. It was postmarked Detroit. I asked aroun' and found out that yo' best friend lives here. The rest was easy."

He makes no attempt to get up. His eyes are hard but I see no flashes of anger in them. His expression reminds me more of a burned-down fire where embers smolder beneath the surface. I know I should get out of here before the embers flare into flames.

"May Lilly, Cherub. Come outside with me. I need to speak to y'all."

May Lilly disengages her arms from her daddy's neck and follows me outside.

Cherub looks at me with defiance and says, "I ain't goin' out there. It's pourin' down rain." She grunts and locks her arms around his neck as she nuzzles his cheek.

The rain beats down, soaking through our clothes. "May Lilly, is it true that you sent him a card?"

She lowers her head and avoids my eyes. Lighting flashes. A sharp clap of thunder makes a ping sound like something close by was struck. "Yes, Ma'am."

My heart sinks to my stomach to think that my little girl betrayed me, risked my life like this. "Don't you remember what he did to us, May Lilly?"

"Yes, Ma'am. But, when you were in the hospital in Atlanta, Daddy promised that he would never hurt us again. Besides, I didn't put our address on it." Her eyes are wide with innocence and fear. Afraid of the storm she's caught in between her daddy and me.

"We can't stay here, May Lilly. Your father is a dangerous man. We'll have to spend the night with Candy and Harold."

I take her hand and try to pull her down the steps. She starts crying and hollering, "I want to stay with Daddy and Cherub. He drove all the way from Georgia to see me. Come on in and look at all the pretty clothes and toys he brought me. Please, Mama. Please! Can't we just stay together and be happy tonight?"

He hears and comes to where we're standing just outside the door in the rain. Cherub stands behind him inside the doorway with her hands on her hips, lips pushed out in a pout. She's tall as he is and looks more like a woman than a child.

Anger flashes in his green eyes. "Look here, Baby Heart. I got a right to visit my daughter. You stole her and my money. You got two crimes against you, kidnapping and theft. I can take her back to Georgia if I want to and you can't do a damn thing about it. I got as much right to her as you have. If you bring yo' ass back to Georgia, I'll have you put in jail."

I feel weak. If he takes May Lilly, I'll have none of my children. "Please don't take her," I say. "How long do you plan to be here?"

"We'll just spend the night. Cherub and me are gonna head on back to White Chalk tomorrow. I have a lot of bitniz to take care of."

"You're welcome to spend the night here. I'll stay downstairs. Cherub, why don't you come with me so we'll have some time together before you go back."

She rolls her eyes at me and says, "No, Ma'am. I wanna stay here with May Lilly and Daddy John El."

I can't afford to anger him. I know he has a gun and he can take my daughter. I'm afraid to turn my back. I wait until they go inside and close the door before I run downstairs and ring Candy's doorbell.

Harold opens the door. "Baby Heart, what's the matter? You're drenched and look like you're scared to death."

"You're right about both. Where's Candy?"

"She went to a meeting. Come in. What's wrong?"

"Harold, John El is here. He's upstairs. He has my children up there and there's nothing I can do about it."

Harold stands up. I have never seen him look so alarmed before. "Do you want me to go up there and make him leave?"

"Harold, I know he has a gun. I don't want to get you and Candy mixed up in this mess. I'm going out to Morrie's in Oak Park. I just wanted ya'll to know he's up there. May Lilly and Cherub are with him. It's not like he's holding them hostage. They refused to leave with me. They love their daddy and want to be with him."

"Okay. But if I hear any strange sounds, I'll go up there or call the police."

I take a quick look at the steps leading to the upper flat before I rush through the pouring rain to my car. I have a key in case Morrie isn't home. What a way to celebrate my graduation, I think. My mind is in turmoil. I don't believe he will hurt May Lilly or Cherub. But there's nothing to prevent him from taking May Lilly with him.

Something else is gnawing at my mind — the way he and Cherub are acting. She's way too grown to be sitting on his lap and snuggling with him. I sense something more than a father-daughter relationship between them. He's getting back at me by using my dead sister's child who is like my own. It's a low-down dirty trick John El is pulling. But I don't know if I can do anything about it.

Why didn't he bring Joel? I wondered about that right away but I was too frightened to ask.

It's six in the evening when I arrive at Morrie's house in Oak Park. He's at home. I catch him in between his shift at the market and the nightclubs. He's shocked and furious when I tell him what's going on.

His first expression is outrage. "I'll go over there and kill the bastard with my bare hands."

I calm myself and take his hands in mine. "Morrie, you must not go over there. It would be bad for you and the children."

Morrie rubs his forehead. "I'll call a lawyer. Maybe we can have him arrested."

Before I know it, Morrie is on the phone talking to one of his lawyers.

After he hangs up, he shakes his head slowly and says, "There's not much we can do if the courts haven't awarded custody. He's right. Under Michigan and Georgia law, he has as much right to Joel and May Lilly as you do."

"Even after he tried to kill me?"

"Because you didn't press charges, there is no record of spouse abuse or attempted murder. Unless he assaulted you since he arrived in Michigan, there's nothing can be done on that account."

I wring my hands and burst into tears, "You mean he can just walk out of there with my child?"

"There's nothing can be done legally." Morrie wipes my tears away with his thumb. "I'll be damned if I'll allow him to take my only grandchild."

"What are you going to do?"

"You stay here. I have to meet with my lawyer. Then I'll get in touch with a friend on the police force. Mr. Murphy may be a big shot where he comes from. But he's on my turf now."

 38

MORRIE SWINGS INTO ACTION

An hour after Morrie leaves, he calls back and tells me, "Rest easy, Daughter. I have a police detective watching your flat. If he tries to leave with May Lilly, he will be followed and arrested before he gets out of the city limits."

"I thought they couldn't arrest him."

"Not for taking May Lilly. They can arrest him for a traffic violation. They'll search him and if he's carrying a concealed weapon without a Michigan permit, they'll lock him up. While he's in custody, they will call you to pick up your daughter."

Morrie clears his throat and continues slowly. "If that doesn't work, he's traveling with an unrelated female minor. They can hold him while they contact the Georgia authorities to determine if he has permission of her father or legal guardian to transport her across state lines. Based on your observations, he may be molesting her. They can detain him and question the girl. If it's true they can hold him on several charges."

"I'm relieved you have police watching the house. But I don't know if I want to get Cherub involved with the authorities on suspicion of him molesting her. If I'm wrong, she'll never forgive me. Let me call and try to talk with her."

"You know best how to handle a situation like this. But rest assured the policeman will find a way to detain him if he tries to leave Detroit with May Lilly. Let me know what you want to do about your niece."

"Okay." I hang up and dial my home phone number. May Lilly answers. I can tell she was in the middle of a giggle when she says, "Hello."

"May Lilly, are you okay?"

"Yes, Ma'am. I'm having fun with Daddy and Cherub. We're playing a game Daddy brought me. He's not mad with you. Come up here with us."

"No, I can't. You have fun. Let me talk to Cherub." I don't let her know that I'm not downstairs with Candy.

Cherub comes to the phone. The tone of her voice is edged with irritation. "Hey, Aunt Baby Heart. What do you want?"

"I haven't seen you in so long. I just wanted to talk with you. Let you know I love you and how much I've missed you."

"If you love me so much, how come you ran off and left me with Willie Lee?"

"Baby, I wanted to bring you and Joel with me. Willie Lee went to the police and got a court order to get you while I was in the hospital in Atlanta. I could have been arrested for kidnapping if I had taken you without his permission."

"Did you ask him if I could come?"

"No. I was running for my life. Don't you remember the day John El shot Joel and me? You were there. I almost died. I had to get away from him, Cherub."

"You don't know what I've been through with Willie Lee. He's drunk all the time and beats me. If it wasn't for Daddy John El, I would have starved to death."

I feel deep sorrow for her, caught between two abusive men, forced to choose between the lesser of the two evils from her point of view. "Cherub, did you get the letters and gifts I sent to you?"

"No."

"I wrote to you every week since I've been here and sent birthday and Christmas presents."

"I don't believe you sent me nothin'. I remember before my mama died. Willie Lee beat her and starved us and you never came to see us or brought a crumb of food."

"Cherub, you were too young to remember what happened before Irene died. You should remember that I loved and raised you like my own child until I was shot.

"I want to know about you and John El," I say to Cherub, changing the subject.

"What about us?"

"I told you when you were ten years old that you shouldn't sit on his lap anymore. Yesterday you were on his lap and he seemed to be enjoying it. It's just not proper. Has he touched you on your breast or private parts?"

"You got a dirty mind. You just jealous because he don't want you no mo'. I don't want to talk with you." She slams the phone down in my ear.

I call Morrie back and tell him not to report my suspicions about Cherub and John El to the police. I'm satisfied he isn't molesting her.

Morrie says, "I'm not convinced, but if you say so."

"I just think it's best for her if we leave it alone. He never touched me before we were married. So maybe he's not bothering her."

"I don't want you to go home while he's still there. How do you plan to get May Lilly?"

"I'll go over to Candy's tomorrow morning and call May Lilly, ask her to come downstairs. If she doesn't come, can I have the police bring her down to me?"

"Afraid not. They can't do that because you don't have legal custody. But if he puts her in the car, they will follow and arrest him like I said before."

I arrive at Candy's house before day.

At 7 A.M before I call her, the doorbell rings. May Lilly waves goodbye to her daddy and Cherub. I breathe a sigh of relief as I watch them walk down the street to his car. I'm still worried for Cherub but I didn't want them to have a confrontation with the police.

The first thing I plan to do next week is talk with Morrie's lawyer about a divorce and getting legal custody of May Lilly.

39

LIFE KEEPS MOVING INTO THE FUTURE

After my encounter with John El, Morrie insists that May Lilly and I move to Oak Park with him so we will be safer. I know he's right but I miss Candy. It was fun living upstairs from my best friend. Now I have to drive miles when I want to see her. Sometimes she and Harold come to see us.

Morrie says if John El ever comes to his home, he will leave in handcuffs or an ambulance. It hurts to see the sadness in May Lilly's eyes when we explain to her that she can't tell her daddy where we live, invite him to visit or send him cards postmarked from Oak Park. I make one concession. I allow her to phone him on Sunday evenings. I listen in on the calls on the extension phone. In exchange, John El allows me to speak to Joel.

Nobody says so, but I know he's listening when I talk to Joel.

"Hey, Mama." Joel says.

The first time I hear his voice in more than two years, I'm so happy I want to jump through the phone. "Hey Joel! How are you, Son?"

"Just fine." His voice is low and guarded. There's no spark of joy in it. I feel a tear slide down my face.

"Why didn't you come to Detroit with John El and Cherub?"

"I stayed to oversee the store and chalk mine."

"Joel, you're only twelve."

"Daddy taught me how to run things. He's turning everything over to me when I get grown," he says proudly.

"Where did you stay while they were away?"

John El interrupts, "Ya'll done talked about long enough. Tell your mama goodnight, Joel."

Once I asked John El if we could include Cherub in the Sunday night calls and he says, "What makes you think she's here?"

"I thought she spends time with you and Joel."

"Well you thought dead wrong. She lives with Willie Lee. I brought her to Detroit to give her a little enjoyment and you treated us both like dirt."

I can tell he's getting worked up. I never ask about her again. But I have a nagging feeling still. I remember how he used to love for me to sit on his lap in baby doll pajamas. An image leaps in mind of Cherub sitting on his lap like that. I shake my head and make it go away. Maybe I do have a dirty mind. She's just a little girl and John El is over fifty years old now. Surely he doesn't have a romantic interest in a girl that young, especially one he helped raise. I feel guilty about my thoughts and hope John El is making sure she's fed and okay.

Enrollment in Marygrove College is a highlight of my life. I'm on the path to becoming a nurse. My dream is finally coming true. I settle into college life and my new home in Oak Park. Because of segregation and racism, I make no new friends in Oak Park. The neighbors assume I'm Morrie's housekeeper. Whatever they think is their business. As long as they don't bother us, we don't bother them and life goes on.

 *40*

MAY 1961

THE INVITATION

Mail is still transferred to me in Oak Park from my old address. I look idly at the Georgia postmark, drop the mail on the kitchen table and get on with cooking. After we've had dinner and the dishes have been washed and put away, I sit down to open the mail. The mail from Georgia, without a return address, looks like it may be a birthday card or invitation.

I tear open the envelope and find another envelope. I open it and the words pop out at me in a jumble. I can't wrap my brain around the message.

Cordially invited. Cherry Johnson. Daughter of. June 15,1961. You are. Willie Lee Johnson. The late Irene Turner Johnson. To John El Murphy.

Who is Cherry Johnson? I read it over again, slowly. It's a wedding invitation. I'm being invited to John El's wedding to someone named Cherry. She's the daughter of — now it hits me hard like Joe Louis punched me in the stomach — Willie Lee Johnson and the late Irene Turner Johnson, my sister.

Cherry is Cherub's given name. We've called her Cherub Murphy so long; I've forgotten her real name is Cherry Johnson.

John El is a dirty dog! I can't believe he's doing this. And he has the nerve to invite me. I don't think I make a sound. I'm just sitting here staring at this disgusting invitation when May Lilly asks me, "What's wrong, Mama?"

"Nothing, baby. Nothing. I just received an invitation to a wedding."

"Who's getting married, Mama?"

"An old friend of mine I went to school with in Marysville. You don't know her."

I don't want May Lilly to learn about this disgusting affair. How am I supposed to tell my daughter that her father is marrying her first cousin who she considers her sister and who is only four years older than her.

I get up and walk to my bedroom slow and deliberately, like an old lady. Still in a state of shock, I hide the invitation.

After May Lilly is asleep, I tell Morrie about it.

He holds his hands together in a way that resembles a prayer posture, looks at me solemnly and asks, "What are we going to do?"

265

"What can we do? Georgia law allows a girl to marry at her age if her father signs for it. I'm sure Willie Lee has given his permission. He would sign her into white slavery for a bottle of wine."

"That child has no notion of what she's doing, Jolee. We have to rescue her before she ends up in worse danger than she's already in."

"I know. I have to do something to save her. I just don't know how to go about it. I'll call my brother, Lincoln, and see if he can talk her out of it, maybe bring her up here."

"Try that. If it doesn't work, we'll try something else. There's usually more than one way to solve a problem. We'll start with the easiest way first."

I phone Lincoln. "Did you get an invitation to your niece's wedding?

"Na. I ain't got no invitation. Which one of my niece's gettin' married?"

"I'm surprised they would invite me but not you and Papa Joe."

"Who the hell you talkin' about, Baby Heart?"

"Cherub, that's who. I just got an invitation to her June fifteenth wedding to John El Murphy."

I hear his breath coming in quick angry gasps. I imagine the vein throbbing at his temple. "Oh, hell no! Not after what he done to you. He's plannin' to take my little niece and mess up her life. He's old enough to be her granddaddy. The thought of it is disgustin'. I'll shoot him down like a dog before I let it happen."

"Keep a cool head, Lincoln. Go up there and try to talk her out of it. If she's determined, maybe you can talk to Willie Lee. Offer him money to take back his permission. I'll pay him."

"Willie Lee don't speak to me since I kicked his ass the day he came to the cemetery when we buried Irene. It's useless to say anything to him. He'd be scared to go back on his word to John El, anyhow. I think I should just go on and kill John El. I shoulda killed him a long time ago. Seems like he just got to keep screwin' aroun' with my family."

"Take Papa Joe with you. Ask him to talk some sense into Cherub before it's too late. You can't just kill John El in cold blood, Linc."

"My blood ain't cold. It's boilin' hot. But I'll try it yo' way and call you back after we go to White Chalk."

Lincoln calls back the following week. "We went to White Chalk."

"What did Cherub say?"

"We never got to see her. We went up to Willie Lee's. Nobody was home. We even went down in the woods lookin' for him. He wasn't at the still. So we went to John El's. Nobody was there. We went over to Rose's. She got a invitation. Says she ain't seen Cherub in ages. She heard that she spends most of her time with John El and Joel."

"I figured John El was lying to me when he said Cherub wasn't staying with them."

"Anyhow, I went on down to the store." Linc continued. "Neither John El nor Cherub was there. His worker said they all went to Macon or Atlanta shoppin'. It's a good thing. If he'd been there, I probably would have laid his ass to rest."

"I have a plan, Lincoln. Listen carefully. I'm coming to the wedding. This is what I want you to do. And it doesn't involve bloodshed."

Morrie encourages me to attend the wedding and offers his help, "I'm sending Rocky with you. He will be your driver and bodyguard."

I have met Rocky. He's the bouncer at Morries' Flamingo Night Club. Black as midnight with a clean-shaven head, Rocky is a mountain of a man with muscles like boulders. Morrie told me once that Rocky did time in the penitentiary for manslaughter. Nobody messes with Rocky Steele. Morrie trusts him to get me down there and back safely with Cherub.

 *41*

THE WEDDING

JUNE 1961

The long ride to Georgia is quiet. Rocky doesn't talk more than is absolutely necessary.

I wanted to drive my yellow Cadillac or rent a limousine. I envisioned making a big splash when we drive up to John El's house where the wedding is being held. Both Morrie and Rocky nixed that idea.

Morrie had said, "We want a car as much like the average automobile on the road in and near White Chalk, as possible. Our mission, after all, is to abduct the bride on her wedding day. We don't want to attract attention or be easy to describe."

Rocky drives while I sit in the backseat of our ordinary five-year old Ford. From the outside it looks average with a few dents, somewhat worn. Under the hood is a shiny new supped up V8 engine, capable of a quick takeoff. All other parts have been replaced with new ones to lessen the possibility of malfunctions such as flat tires or starter failure.

The quietness gives me time to think.

I'm convinced we're doing the right thing although I know it won't be easy. When I married John El, I didn't like him, much less think I was in love with him. I married him because of the promise I made when I was trying to save my mother's life. Cherub is marrying him because she thinks she's in love. He has become her knight in shining armor, protecting her from Willie Lee and his cruelty.

She loved John El as a child growing up in his house. As she entered puberty and continued to sit on his lap and hug him maybe she thought the sexual feelings she experienced with him were normal. But how she goes from father to boyfriend and husband with the same man is insane. I've read and heard enough to believe Cherub has been brainwashed and needs rescue and therapy. I reassure myself. My intentions are pure.

My thoughts turn to John El. I read the newspapers and watch TV. There are stories about kids being molested or raped by grown men. These men are called pedophiles. I believe John El is one. I search my memory all the way back to my early childhood days when I would go to his store. He would come out from behind the counter, give me a penny candy while he stroked my hair. His eyes always took on a strange gleam.

He admitted he had liked me since I was a baby. I remember Bobby Joe asking me 'What kind of grown man likes a baby like a girlfriend?'

when I told him that story. At the time I had answered 'A strange one.' I had no way of knowing then that there was a name for men like him. The really strange part is I don't think John El knows that he's a pervert. He has been able to control himself to the point where his behavior is acceptable, at least in White Chalk where he rules.

I think about the first day he laid eyes on Cherub. It was the day Irene died. He looked at her with that funny gleam in his eyes and remarked on her beauty and pretty hair. He said 'You can bring that one home to live with us.' I remember how he encouraged her to sit on his lap while he stroked her hair. He never did that with May Lilly.

Now I think back to when we first married, how he wanted me to sit on his lap wearing baby doll pajamas and sucking a lollipop, my hair in long braids over each shoulder. It's all so obvious to me now. He was grooming Cherub to take my place as I grew older and he could no longer pretend I was a little girl.

The closer we get to Georgia, the stronger I feel that we're doing the right thing.

"Rocky, I brought the camera. Did you get the press card to hang around your neck?"

"Uh-huh." Rocky grunts.

"We'll stop by Candy's Mama's house first when we get there, so I can change my clothes."

Rocky shakes his massive baldhead from side to side. "Not a good idea. I know a colored owned motel in Atlanta. We'll stop there for an hour. Give us time to shower and change. Timing is important to carry this job off. We have to arrive minutes before the wedding starts. Don't want anyone seeing us ahead of time."

"Did you bring the handcuffs?"

"I got everything I need. And I got everything timed. Just don't spend over an hour getting changed."

When we get to the motel in Atlanta, I hurry up getting ready. I shower, change into a black dress, brush my hair back and pin it up before I slip the black veil over my head and face.

I return to the car where Rocky is waiting and notice that the license plates have been changed from the Great Lakes of Michigan to the Peach state of Georgia.

When we crest the hill leading to John El's estate, where I was held captive for eleven years, I tell Rocky to pull off the road behind a grove of trees. I take binoculars from my purse and peer beyond the peach trees and lilac bushes until I see John El leave the house and walk slowly toward the arbor that will serve as the wedding altar, the same as it did for us fourteen years ago.

I slide into the front seat next to Rocky and tell him, "Now. She's in the dressing room with Queen Esther, the wedding planner. Lincoln will stir her to our car for a wedding photo before she walks down the aisle."

Rocky tries to re-enter the narrow road leading to the house. A string of cars are ahead of us on their way to the wedding.

"Shit! What do we do now?" I ask Rocky in a panic. "We've got to be there before she starts to the altar."

Rocky guns the motor and slides in-between two cars faster than greased lighting. He drives over the grass and pulls to the side of the house just in time for me to see Cherub coming down the steps of the front porch in a ruffled white wedding gown. Except for the wedding veil and train, she looks like a young girl on her way to the Junior Prom.

Willie Lee is on one side of her. Her Matron of Honor, who is a first cousin, is on the other side. I don't see any bridesmaids. She probably doesn't have any girlfriends.

Then I see Lincoln move in front of them and point to Rocky. Lincoln walks ahead to our car, opens the back door and slides in. I move over to the driver's seat. At the same time Rocky walks to the bride with his camera pointed.

The wedding party pauses as Rocky holds up the press card hanging from his neck. I know he's explaining that he's been sent from the Macon Telegraph to cover the wedding. He points to the car. Cherub and Willie Lee follow him.

Rocky positions Cherub and Willie Lee for a photo beside the car, Lincoln opens the back door wide, reaches for her by the long train of her gown and pulls. Rocky shoves her from the front and slides in the backseat next to her. The car door slams shut and I gun the motor. Vroom! Gravel and clay beats against the sides of the car as I speed off down the road. I'm flying but not so fast that I don't see John El when he runs up to where the car was parked and where Willie Lee still stands with his mouth open, looking stunned.

A sound like firecrackers going off fills the air. I realize that it's gunfire. I think he's shooting at our car. I press harder on the gas pedal and look through the rearview mirror. Willie Lee falls to the ground. John El is standing over him with the pistol still pointed at his body.

Rocky has handcuffed Cherub and holds her head down, face pressed against his chest. When we no longer hear shots, he lets her sit up. She screams all kind of curse words and threats at us as we drive toward Marysville. "John El is gonna kill all of you sons-of-bitches. What in the hell do you think you're doin'? Let me out of this goddamned car this minute. This my weddin' day."

When we reach the divide in the road that leads to Sawyersville one way and Marysville the other, we pull into a thicket where Linc left his car and let him out.

I roll down the window and ask him, "What happened back there?"

"I'm not sure. But it looked like he shot Willie Lee."

"Why would he do that?"

"I don't know."

"Thanks for your help, Linc."

"Yeah. I hope you can get the kid straightened out." Then he leans in and whispers in my ear, "I think he killed Willie Lee. I'll let you know what happened."

Rocky changes our plates back to Michigan. I remove my veil and drive carefully, observing all traffic rules so there will be no need for cops to pull us over. If they have been notified of the abduction, they will be looking for Georgia plates.

We forgot one thing that we now wish we had— earplugs. Cherub is screaming at the top of her lungs and calling me every low-down dirty name she's ever heard or thought. Rocky sits in the back holding on to her, making sure she doesn't try to throw herself from the car or kick the backseat out.

We only stop for gas. Rocky holds the back of Cherub's head, pressing her lips to his, so she can't scream while the attendant is in earshot. I stand outside and make small talk, so he doesn't notice her squirming, trying to get away from Rocky. One gas attendant noticed them and said, "Newly weds, huh?"

I nod and give him a knowing smile.

Going in restrooms with a handcuffed bride is out of the question. So we stop alongside the road using the car as a privacy shield. Rocky turns his head and holds on tight to her, while I pull the long cumbersome gown up and panties down so she can pee.

It's late afternoon the following day when we turn into the long driveway of the Haven Home Sanitarium in the suburbs of Detroit. Haven Home is a one- story rambling red brick facility, secluded from the road by giant oak trees. It's a prestigious private mental hospital whose patients are mostly neurotic rich white folks according to Morrie.

The staff looks at us like we all are in need of inpatient care. Cherub in wedding gown and handcuffs is shouting profanities in a hoarse voice; Rocky, a black mountain of a man could use a shave and shower and his patience has clearly been worn to a frazzle; and me in a wrinkled black dress, tangled hair and streaked make-up.

Morrie is a close friend of the chief psychiatrist. He has made arrangements for Cherub's admission ahead of time. Being Morrie he never mentioned race, only that I was his daughter and wanted to admit my niece who has been brainwashed by a pedophile.

The shock on the face of the admissions nurse is unmistakable. "Are you sure you're not looking for Northville State Hospital?" she asks.

"We're in the right place. My father, Mr. Morrie Rubenstein made the arrangements with Dr. Wineman."

"I'll be right back," she says while looking at me like I'm in need of admission quick. She trots off down the hall.

A few minutes later the nurse returns with a man in a white jacket. Dave Wineman, M.D. is stitched on the pocket. His hair is silver gray and crinkles appear around his eyes when he smiles. Doctor Wineman extends his hand and with a pleasant smile says, "How are you, Mrs. Murphy? Morrie has told me about you many times."

"Glad to meet you, doctor. My niece needs help."

"Come with me to my office." He shoots the nurse, who is standing by with her mouth wide open, a dismissive look.

Cherub tries to break away from Rocky. He holds tight. She yells looking at me, "You witch. You're trying to put me in a nuthouse. They kidnapped me, doctor. I don't even know these people. Call the police. They kidnapped me on my weddin' day."

Dr. Wineman pats her shoulder, smiles and looks at her with warm, kind eyes. "You may be right, dear. The sooner you calm down and tell me all about it, the sooner you can be out of here." He turns to me. "Mrs. Murphy, you and the gentleman can leave now. We will handle things and call if we need you."

I look back at Cherub with a lump of sadness in my heart. I hope one day she will understand I had to do this for her own good. Right now, I want to go home, soak in a hot bath and sleep for days.

 *42*

ALL OF MY CHILDREN

After less than an hours' sleep, the shrill ring of the telephone awakens me. I curse under my breath and reach for the phone next to my bed. It's my sister, Rose.

"Baby Heart. You'll never guess what done happened down here."

I yawn, shake my head and try to wake up though I don't want to. "No, I can't guess. What?"

"You in bed already? It's only six in the evening."

"I know the time, Rose. Yes, I was sleeping. What happened?"

"I don't know if you got an invitation but John El and Cherub were supposed to get married Sunday, a big weddin' like yo's. Well, it looks like Willie Lee arranged for somebody to come steal her away right before the weddin'. John El ran up and emptied his pistol into Willie Lee." Rose starts boohooing.

"What are you crying about, Rose?"

"Didn't you hear me? John El killed Willie Lee. And nobody knows where Cherub is. We don't know where to find her to let her know her daddy's dead."

Rose is a good person, stout and usually jolly. She Never thinks badly of anyone, even Willie Lee who kicked our sister Irene in the stomach, killing the last baby he put in her womb and causing her to fill an early grave. "Calm down, Rose. Willie Lee's death isn't entirely unexpected. He was so brutal to Irene that I'm not feeling much sympathy right now."

"Baby Heart, you shouldn't speak unkind about the dead."

"Then I guess we shouldn't talk about Willie Lee at all. What happened to John El?"

"The sheriff came and took him to jail. John El admitted that he shot Willie Lee. He said Willie Lee took his money to give permission for Cherub to marry him and then had her taken away. He kept sayin' 'He tried to make a fool out of me.'"

"Where is John El now?"

"Out on bond. They didn't even keep him in jail overnight."

"Where is my son? Did he witness the killing?"

"Yeah. We all seen it. I took Joel home with me but John El came and got him the next day."

"Do they know who took Cherub away?"

"It was a big bald headed black man, looked like a giant. He pretended to be a reporter from Macon who came to take her picture for the paper. Nobody had ever seen him in these parts before. Somebody told me Linc was there, but he disappeared and we couldn't find him. I called him last night. He's at home. Said he left when he saw there was gonna be trouble."

Lincoln sure knows how to keep his mouth shut, I think. I smile with the realization that nobody saw me or knew I was there, except Linc. Now I say to Rose, "I received an invitation. John El marrying Cherub, who is like a daughter to him, was more than I cared to witness."

"I guess you right. It's kind of nasty when you think about it. Maybe that's why Willie Lee sent her away."

My eyelids droop. I'm worn out from the long, tiring ride from Georgia and admitting Cherub to the hospital. "Rose, I really have to go. I'll call you later."

I climb back into bed and begin to drift off when the phone rings again. It's Doctor Wineman, "I just wanted you to know your niece is going to be fine. We gave her a sedative and she's resting. My work with her will begin tomorrow. I prefer that she have no visitors. It will take a while to get background information, make a diagnosis and begin the treatment process."

I thank him for the call and agree that it's better for us not to visit right now. I try to go back to sleep, but its no use.

Sleep is no longer calling to me. I take a bath; change my clothes and head over to Candy's to get my daughter. At least with Cherub in the hospital, I don't have to explain things to May Lilly.

Joel is heavy on my heart. He's been through so much and now this. If John El is sent to prison maybe I can get my son back. This thought gives me hope that I will have all of my children together again. Maybe some good will come from Willie Lee's death.

Doctor Wineman calls regularly to give me updates on Cherub. He tells me she's making progress. Then about six weeks after I had her admitted, he calls to tell me that she's ready for discharge.

I'm a little nervous as I drive out to Haven Home. I don't know if I can handle the angry teenager I left there. What if she hates me and blames me for what happened to her father and bridegroom.

I have shared the bad news with Dr. Wineman who assured me that it was best for him to handle it in therapy with Cherub.

She looks like an angel sitting serenely by the window, looking out over the rolling green lawn when I enter her room with an attendant. Her sweet repose doesn't last long. When she sees me she bolts from her chair and runs into my arms crying, "Mama, Mama. You've come for me. I didn't think you would want me."

I hold her tight. Then I wipe the tears from her eyes, "Of course I want you. I only left you here so Dr. Wineman could help you understand what happened to you."

"Mama, I'm so ashamed. Please forgive me. How could I do such a thing? He was yo' husban' and my daddy."

"Cherub, you were the victim. I thought Dr. Wineman helped you to understand that."

"He did. But when I look at you, I feel so dirty. I feel like a hussy."

I hug her again. "You're no hussy. You're a normal teenage girl. Whatever you did was to survive. It's all over now. You're my daughter. I love you. Get your things. It's time to go home."

On the way home, we talk about the future. "Cherub, we have to get you ready to enroll in school in the fall."

She lowers her head and says softly, "I ain't been to school in over three years, not since I went to live with Willie Lee. I'm too old to go to school in the same grade with May Lilly. I should be in ninth by now. I quit in sixth grade."

"You're a bright girl. With the help of Candy and I, you may soon be ready for eighth grade. That's only one year behind. Are you willing to work really hard?"

"Yes, Ma'am."

When school starts in September, Cherub tests at eighth grade level. She's having fun with kids her age. She studies hard and goes to ballgames and parties. She's experiencing a world that she never knew existed when she was in White Chalk. Cherub thanks me almost every day for giving her a chance to live a normal life.

I tell her, "Cherub, you don't need to thank me. If anything I should thank you for giving me a second chance to be the kind of mother you deserve."

She's beautiful and sweet most of the time. No teenager is perfect. I have to get on her to keep her room clean and she's not allowed to hang out after curfew. I have to know any guys she keeps company with.

But I'm blessed that she's level headed and thinking about a future as a social worker after she finishes high school and goes on to college.

I hear from Linc and Rose often. John El was tried and convicted of killing Willie Lee. He was sentenced to five to ten years in the penitentiary for manslaughter. People in White Chalk are betting that he will be out in less than two years.

Joel refuses to come live with us in Detroit. I still beg him to come but his answer is always the same, "Mama if I leave, everything Daddy worked so hard for will be lost."

"But, Joel you're a child. The chalk mine is not your responsibility. You should be with me and your sisters."

"I'm thirteen. Jesus went about his father's business when he was only twelve."

"How did you know that, Joel?"

"I still read the Bible, like you taught me."

I want to argue that he's not Jesus and this is a different time and place than Jesus' day. But he's so serious. He sounds like a man. I can't bring myself to force him to leave what he feels is his calling. Instead I make a deal with him. I allow him to stay on in White Chalk and oversee his father's businesses if Papa Joe will come and live in the house with him and provide supervision while John El is in prison. He agrees and Papa Joe is willing. So it's done.

We make plans to return to White Chalk for Christmas. I will see my son for the first time in three years. I tremble with excitement and joy at the anticipation of having my family all together again without fear of John El.

 *43*

CHRISTMAS IN WHITE CHALK

DECEMBER 1961

It's been a long time since Papa Joe and I went into the woods and picked out a Christmas tree. I daydream about reliving my childhood as we drive toward Georgia for the holidays. Morrie and I drive while May Lilly and Cherub entertain each other in the backseat. Candy and Harold are following us in their car.

Papa Joe meets us at the front door when we arrive tired and worn from our long journey. He wraps me in his arms that are not as strong as I remember but the warmth and love in his embrace are unmistakable. "Baby Heart! I been watchin' the road all day. Waitin' for y'all to make it in."

"We got here as fast as we could, Papa Joe. Even with the new interstate highways, it's a fourteen hour drive." I notice more gray than black in the long braids hanging over each of his shoulders. And his eyes, that used to be clear with pupils dark and sparkling like black diamonds, are now dull.

He hugs May Lilly and Cherub then extends his hand to Morrie in welcome. They greet each other like two old friends. They met two summers ago when Papa Joe and Linc visited us in Detroit.

Papa Joe knows that Morrie considers himself my father but he's not jealous in the least. He understands that no one can replace him. Not many people have two fathers who love them the way Papa Joe and Morrie love me.

They are unusual companions, my two fathers, from different religions, cultures, races and experiences. Yet they seem to have so much to talk about. I watch the two elderly men sitting before the fire, one black with long braids speaking in broken English, the other small and wiry, speaking impeccable English with a few Yiddish expressions thrown in. I am the only thing they have in common. I suppose they are learning from each other.

"Papa Joe, how about us going into the woods to find a pretty Christmas tree tomorrow?" I ask, interrupting their conversation.

His eyes brighten. "I think I know just where to find a right pretty one in a thicket close to the old place. What time you want to go?"

"I'm gonna turn in early so we can go first thing in the morning."

I choose the big bedroom that John El and I shared when we were married. I toss and turn and can't close my eyes. He may be in prison but I feel his presence in this room. His mean green eyes are looking down on me, following my every move.

Morrie is in the first guest bedroom. That's the room where I changed into my wedding dress that looked like little Bo Peep's pinafore. Papa Joe and Joel are in the bedroom that John El kept locked with his illegal money behind the walls. This house has too many bad memories.

Finally, I curl up on the old Victorian sofa in the living room with my pearl handled revolver under my head. I don't trust prison to hold John El Murphy. Once a bullet pierces your heart and you live to tell it, trust is replaced by fear. I'm afraid if I sleep, I will awaken with John El standing over me. So I dose fitfully through the night.

Papa Joe, May Lilly and I drive up to the old homestead where I was born and raised in search of the perfect Christmas tree. Joel was invited but declined. He thinks Christmas trees are childish. He's spending Christmas Eve overseeing the store.

Morrie went with Joel. He wants to compare the store to his market in Detroit, maybe give Joel a pointer or two about management.

We approach the old house. It was never more than a shack and is falling down now. I feel sorry for it, standing abandoned and forlorn. Unpainted gray boards stick out in different directions like broken bones. The old oak tree that I love still stands near my bedroom window, that has no glass — just a gapping hole. May Lilly looks at it and shudders with fear. But this is home for me. I feel love.

I park the car and we walk into the woods. Papa Joe has the axe slung over his shoulder. I notice that his once broad shoulders stoop and his steps are halting. Before we walk very far, he stops and pants for breath.

"Papa Joe, are you okay? Here, let me carry that axe."

"I'm all right. Just old age, Baby Heart." He holds his chest as he bends over.

"I don't know, Papa Joe. Maybe I should take you to the doctor."

"Now, I done tole you. Nothin' wrong with me but ole age and a touch of arthritis. Nothin' to go gittin' worked up ovah. Sittin' in a doctor's office ain't gonna change nothin'."

"Okay, Papa Joe if you say so." I pick a tree quickly, so as not to prolong the walk.

"Baby Heart, you sho this is the one?"

He always asked me that when I was a kid. "Yes, Sir. This one is perfect." I hug him before I give the tree a whack with the axe. He doesn't insist on cutting it himself. I think something is wrong with Papa Joe and it's more than old age.

Peace prevails on Christmas day. There is no John El Murphy or Willie Lee Johnson to spoil our happiness. We sing Christmas Carols and praise the Lord. Morrie joins in. Even though he's Jewish, he doesn't object to celebrating Jesus' birthday.

The house overflows with family and friends. Rose and her family, Linc, all of Irene's children who are now grown and married with kids, Candy, Harold and her mother join us for Christmas dinner.

Rose and Candy help me prepare the gigantic meal of two turkeys and a goose; oyster stuffing, candied yams, greens, macaroni and cheese, cranberry sauce, and corn bread. Candy's mama and Rose bring enough cakes and pies with them to feed an army. We set up extra tables to accommodate fifty people.

Before dinner the children get to roughhousing. I notice Joel is nervous. So I bundle the kids up and send them outside to play. Joel is worried about the furniture getting scuffed and having to answer to his daddy. I imagine John El walking into the house —filled with my relatives and friends—pulling out his gun and blowing us all into the great beyond. His shadow is ever present.

Even though we could stay longer, I decide to leave the next day. I can't rest in this house where bad memories and an evil spirit dwells.

 *44*

EASTER 1962

It's not that every Easter is bad. It's just that when bad things happen in my life, like death, it's at Easter time, the time when new life is all around in remembrance of our risen Christ. I don't know why it happens this time of year for me.

Tears spill from my eyes onto Papa Joe's cold ashen face. Morrie stands with his arm around my shoulders. Then he gently guides me to my seat in the front row. I'm the last of Papa Joe's big family to be seated before the funeral service begins.

When the casket is slowly closed, I know this is the last time I will see his face in its earthly form. I feel like my heart is being ripped from my chest. A scream escapes my lips. The church nurse rushes to my side with a fan, tissue and smelling salts in case I faint. Linc is on one side of me holding my hand and crying. Morrie is holding my other hand and whispering words of comfort.

My composure has been mostly regained when I see him walk up the aisle and squeeze into the pew next to Joel. Why in the hell did they release him from prison to attend Papa Joe's funeral, I wonder. I tremble and whisper to Morrie, "John El just walked in. He's sitting next to Joel." Morrie nods and holds my hand tighter.

At the cemetery, I stand between Linc and Morrie and watch in pain as clods of red Georgia clay are sprinkled across Papa Joe's casket. When he is lowered into the ground, I tell Morrie I want to leave for Detroit.

We move quickly through the mass of mourners and get in the rental car without taking time to say goodbye. Cherub is with us. I have no idea what is going through John El's mind. I can't risk my fate and the welfare of my children to a demented serial killer.

I know in my heart there are at least two other victims, his first wife who disappeared, and Rosie Petunia who conveniently died a week before she was to receive her inheritance. John El killed them as sure as the sun rises in the East and sets in the West.

By driving above the speed limit to the Atlanta Airport, we are able to get an earlier flight. On the return to Detroit my nerves are a jangle. Morrie sits next to me and I lean my head on his shoulder. This brings looks of anger and disgust from nearby passengers.

People are not ready for interracial couples or old men with young women. I can tell by the looks on their faces that they think we're romantically involved. Morrie insisted that we fly to save time and the hardship of driving in the segregated South where we can't stop for food or use restrooms. And having a white man along could jeopardize our lives.

"How do you think he was able to come to the funeral?" Morrie asks after the plane takes off. The girls are sitting across the aisle out of earshot.

"It's not unusual for prisoners to be allowed to come to funerals of close relatives in the South. But Papa Joe is not related to him anymore. And if he were still a prisoner, he would have been handcuffed to a guard. He strutted in alone as free as the wind."

Morrie holds my hand and gently massages it. He looks directly into my eyes and says, "Jolee, you've had so much trouble in your short life. If one wish could be granted that would bring you happiness, what would it be?"

I frown and try to think. "I would wish to have Joel with us and all of my children grow up to be good, healthy people."

Morrie gives me his wise old fatherly look, shakes his head and says "Spoken like a true mother. But there is a problem. You made two wishes. Only one can be granted. Besides, we both know Joel will not be happy in Detroit. Your wish, if fulfilled, can't make others unhappy."

"Many years ago, I fell in love with a boy. His name is Bobby Joe Miller. For a long time I wished to find him, marry him and live happily ever after. But I learned that wishes don't always come true. Now my hopes are on my children and becoming a nurse."

"What happened to your young man?"

"I don't know. I married John El. He dropped out of school and joined the army. Last I heard he settled somewhere overseas after he was discharged."

Morrie clears his throat. "You know, Jolee, paying my last respects to your papa started me thinking about my own mortality."

"Where are you going with this, Morrie? I can't take any more bad news."

"I don't have bad news. But we all are going to die. I want my house to be in order when I go. I didn't think it proper to ask while Joe was alive and maybe I'm off base to ask now, so stop me if you think what I'm about to propose is inappropriate."

'Propose.' My mind is still jumbled. What the hell is Morrie talking about, I wonder. I hope he isn't hitting on me after all these years of acting like a father. I can't bear to lose two fathers in one day.

"Out with it, Morrie," I say, turning my head to the window to look at the clouds below us that remind me of meringue on a lemon pie.

"I want to make it official, Jolee. I want to adopt you. Will you become my daughter?"

My head is reeling. I draw a deep breath and let it out slowly. "Morrie, I'm a grown woman with children. How are you going to adopt me?"

"I checked it out with my lawyer. I can legally adopt you as long as you consent."

"What's the point? We already consider ourselves father and daughter. A piece of paper won't make us love each other more."

"No, it won't. But it will protect you. If I leave everything I have to you at my death, I'm afraid my will may be contested. If you are legally my daughter it will be less likely that my wishes will be disputed."

"If you think it's necessary, I will consent. But I want you to know that my love for you isn't based on inheriting anything. You've done more for me already than I deserve."

"There is something I want you to do for me," he says seriously.

I turn my face to the window again and think, Oh God, here it comes. I knew Morrie was too good to be true.

His eyes blink and wrinkles appear on his forehead, it seems, from the effort of concentration. "I have always wanted to visit Rome Italy. Will you go with me? I'm afraid that I've waited too late to make a trip like that alone. I would feel more comfortable if you came with me in case I become ill."

"Morrie, I have never traveled abroad. In fact I've only been to a few cities in Georgia and Detroit. And this is my first trip on a plane. I don't know if I'm ready to fly across a ocean."

"Please think about it. You would be doing an old man a big favor. I'm sure Candy will keep the girls if we were to go for a week or two this summer."

I trace the age spots on his hand gently and say, "I'll think about it, Morrie."

I call Linc as soon as we get home. "I'm sorry I couldn't tell ya'll goodbye before we left but I saw John El come in. I didn't want to give him opportunity to commit more murders. No telling what he would have done if he had come face to face with Cherub and me."

"Yeah. We all understand why ya'll left so quick. It's for the best. I heard some busy bodies whisperin' 'bout you an' Morrie; Callin' him yo' sugar daddy. I got 'em straight."

"Folks can sure be cruel. But tell me why John El was allowed to come to the funeral."

"People in White Chalk was bettin' he would only make two years for killin' Willie Lee. Well, they lost their bets. He only made ten months. When he found out Papa Joe was dead, he went to the warden and begged for early parole. I hear he told them there was no one to take care of his minor son, seein' that the child's granddaddy, who was takin' care of him, died an' his no good mama ran away and abandoned him."

"You don't mean he said that about me."

"That's what I heard he said. Anyway, the warden checked with the authorities in White Chalk and Marysville. They said John El shouldn't had to serve one day for killin' the likes of Willie Lee, a worthless drunken nigger who spent his time moon shinin'. So they convened a emergency meetin' of the parole board and John El was out in time for the funeral."

"That sure was fast. Do you think money changed hands?"

"Possible. It sure didn't hurt that his uncle, Doctor Scott, is on the parole board. Course, nobody at the hearin' knew 'bout that connection 'cept John El and the doctor."

I think I will go to Rome.

I owe Morrie a chance to make his one wish come true. Candy and Harold will stay with the girls at Morrie's house. I wouldn't want John El to make an unexpected visit to Detroit thinking I still live with Candy and find my girls there.

 *45*

SOMEWHERE IN THE HEART OF ROME

JULY 1962

All the way to Italy, Morrie talks about how much he wants to visit the Tivoli Fountain in Rome. "Jolee, remember the song Frank Sinatra sings, "Three Coins in the Fountain?"

"Sure. It's one of my favorite songs or was until I stopped believing in magic. I studied up on Rome. I'm more interested in seeing the Catacombs and the Colosseum where the Christians were fed to the lions."

He shakes his head in disbelief. "That is so morbid. Don't you still have interest in love and romance?"

"No. But if you want to go, I'll go with you and watch you toss coins into the fountain. Who knows, maybe you'll regain your youth, meet a beautiful Italian lady and fall in love."

The first day, I insist on visiting the Vatican. I ride in the largest elevator on earth to the Sistine Chapel where I look up in awe at the paintings of Michael Angelo. In St. Peter's Basilica, I study the large bronze statue of St. Peter. Best of all is the Pieta, the statue of the Virgin Mother holding Jesus in her arms and grieving over his dead body. It brings me to tears. Visiting Rome and learning more about what the early Christians suffered strengthens my faith. I feel sort of like I was there suffering with them, bearing the cross with Jesus. Like Jesus, I've had my crosses to bear.

Sometimes it's hard to maintain my Christian spirit when Italian men sneak up behind and pinch me. I have heard they consider this a compliment to a woman's beauty. But I'm not interested in their flirtatious pranks and ask Morrie to walk behind to keep them from touching me.

On our third day in Rome, after we leave the Colosseum and stroll along the streets on our way to dinner, I agree to go with Morrie to visit the fountain. After all, the trip is to fulfill his wish and here I've been dragging him around to Christian sites of interest. I forget that Morrie is Jewish; he's so patient with me.

Over dinner, I try to sound excited. "Morrie, tomorrow is our big day. We'll toss coins in the fountain and wish for our dreams to come true."

"Only make one wish, Jolee. If you make more than one, they will void out each other and none will come true."

"Oh, Morrie. Sometimes I think you really believe that stuff. What are you going to wish for?"

"I can't tell you. It has to be a secret or it won't come true."

The next day after breakfast we head for Tivoli Square. I can sense the excitement in Morrie. He straightens his shoulders and stands tall. He smiles as we approach the gate. I see much more to do in the square than visit the fountain. The garden is beautiful. Flowers are planted in various designs circling the square, showing off God's natural beauty and the artistic creativity of humans. The brilliance of colors— deep purple against lavender, yellow, gold and russet, blues of various hues mesmerizes me. I'm content to bask in the sun and stroll through the beautiful garden. But Morrie urges me on toward the fountain.

He looks nervously at his watch and says, "We need to move on."

"Why? Do we need to be there at a certain time?"

The sound of music drifts through the air from a carousel of many colors, carrying laughing children on brightly painted horses moving up and down. I feel like a kid again and want to capture a childhood I never really had. I look wistfully toward the amusement park area and say, "Let's ride the merry-go-round, Morrie."

He looks annoyed as he pulls me along. "You can come back later. I really want to make my wish before noon."

I think he's acting a little odd but hurry along with him to the fountain. It really is beautiful. Cascades of water shoot up in plumes, reflected through prisms of multicolored, iridescent light, and fall back down. People are standing around the circular fountain edging closer, waiting to get a chance to toss in a coin and make a wish. When we reach the front, I become enthralled by the many coins glistening at the bottom of the fountain. I don't see Morrie when he tosses in his coin, shut his eyes and makes a wish.

He nudges me. "It's your turn, Jolee. Throw a coin in, then close your eyes and make your wish."

Caught up in the mood of excitement, I fish around in my wallet for a dime. I find one, toss and watch as it settles to the bottom among the many other gleaming coins.

With my eyes shut tight, I make my wish: Bobby Joe, please come back to me.

Strong hands slip over my closed eyes. At first, I'm annoyed thinking it's one of the flirtatious Italian men. But the feel of the hands are comforting and familiar, hands from my past. I have felt these hands before.

"Guess who."

The deep rich voice sinks in and I scream, "Bobby Joe — Bobby Joe Miller, is it you?"

The hands move from my eyes. I'm temporarily blinded by sun as I turn to face the man. My vision clears. It's him. I'm standing face to face with the love of my life. He's an older version. The shoulders are broader. He's a bit taller and his hair is mixed like salt and pepper. His face, no longer soft and sweet like a boy, is rugged from time and experience. Lines appear on the brow and around the mouth showing some suffering has carved its niche there. He is more handsome for it.

We fall into each other's arms without a word being spoken.

Voices shouting, "Amore" and sounds of applause bring us down to earth. We move away from the crowd. I look around for Morrie but he's nowhere in sight. We walk arm in arm to a sidewalk café.

At the risk of breaking this magic spell, I ask questions, "Bobby Joe, what are you doing here in the heart of Rome? How did you find me?"

"I wish I could say that it was I who sought you out and found you. But it was your friend or should I say father, Morrie Rubenstein who found me."

"I should have known. He had this all planned and set up. But how did he find you?"

"Through a detective agency. He can give you the details. I don't want to spend our time on that."

A waiter comes over with a menu. Bobby orders Chianti for the table. We sip wine and drink in each other's presence.

"How long have you been here?" I ask him.

"I re-enlisted in the service and attained the rank of Lieutenant. I was stationed here when I met a lovely Italian girl and married her. I have lived here for the last ten years."

I search for a clue to his present marital status. There is a ring on his finger. My heart sinks. Why would Morrie find him and re-unite us if he's married, I wonder.

"Are you happily married?" I ask and hold my breath, not knowing if I want to hear the answer.

"My wife was killed in an automobile accident six months ago." His eyes cloud over as with pain. "I won't lie to you. I was in love with her and very happily married."

I reach for his hand. "I'm sorry, Bobby Joe. I mean I'm sorry for your loss. But I'm glad you had a happy life with her."

Bobby Joe holds onto my hand. His touch sends warm shivers down my spine. "I heard about what happened to you" he says. "I'm sorry you went through so much hell. Sorry I couldn't have protected you and handled your problems but I was only a kid at the time. We both did what we thought we had to do. I couldn't bear living in Georgia while you were with him. That's why I joined the army and never came back, except for my mother's funeral."

"Do you have children, Bobby?"

"One daughter. She's beautiful. Eight years old, the spitting image of her mother. How about you?"

"I have three children. Well, I gave birth to two. I'm raising my niece and my daughter. My son lives in White Chalk with his father."

I want Bobby Joe back in my life. I rush ahead and ask "What are your plans for the future?"

He raises his wine glass in a toast and says, "That depends on you."

"Bobby Joe, do you still love me? Do you feel what I'm feeling?"

"I can only guess what you feel. I know it must still be strong if you impressed someone to search the world for me. When I saw you today, it felt like when we first met at Marysville High and I asked you to be my girl. There has never been a day since then when I didn't think of you. I never stopped loving you, Jolee and I never will."

"I love you, Bobby Joe Miller, from the first day I laid eyes on you. I've never stopped."

He looks deep into my eyes. "Then I only have one question. Will you be my wife?"

"Yes! Oh my God, yes. So long I've waited for this day."

We finish lunch quickly and return to the hotel where I'm staying. I stop by Morrie's room but he's not in. The message light is blinking when we enter my suite. I call the front desk. The message is from Morrie. "Have fun kid. Don't wait up for me. I have a hot date with an Italian beauty."

Bobby and I can't take our eyes and hands off each other. He undresses me and I undress him. We embrace and kiss all the way to the bed. We make love fast with passion. Then, slow and easy until our bodies speed up their thrusting and explode together. I see colors and sights I've never seen before while drifting in another galaxy. It's not easy to regain fourteen years of being apart but I have the best time of my life while we try.

He turns the radio on to a local music station. Sinatra is crooning, "Three Coins in the Fountain." I've found my true love in the heart of Rome, blessed by the fountain and Morrie Rubenstein.

Twilight is descending over the ancient city when we arouse from our lovemaking and a nap in each other's arms. Bobby Joe notices my hotel suite for the first time. He frowns and says, "These are mighty fancy digs you're staying in, Baby Heart. I may not be able to support you in the style to which you've grown accustomed."

"Don't worry. I can't afford this. We got it because of a fluke. We reserved two single rooms. The hotel overbooked and only had one single room left and this suite. Morrie insisted that I take it. They let me have it at the same price the single room would have cost."

"In that case we might as well enjoy it," he says.

The suite is lavish. A dining room and kitchen are located off the entry hall. The living room, bedroom- with a king sized bed- and walk-in closet is down a winding staircase on the lower level. A mahogany bar, stocked with liquor, wine and brandy, runs the length of the living room wall.

The spacious bathroom, decorated in earth tones, has a large ornate tub and a shower.

I turn on the water with intentions of engaging in some steamy sex play in the warm luxurious shower with Bobby Joe. Ten minutes later the water is still ice cold. I turn the knobs and run water in the tub, same result. I call the front desk to inquire why I have no hot water. The desk clerk can't understand me. Bobby Joe speaks to him in Italian, and then he turns to me and says, "Sorry, Baby Heart. The boiler operators are on strike. He's sending up a kettle so we can heat water on the stove. Either that or a cold shower," he laughs. "Welcome to Rome where some group strikes everyday."

We opt for heating water and pouring it in the tub, which takes a long time. But we don't want our ardor cooled by a cold shower. I laugh and say "This reminds me of White Chalk and how I grew up heating water for my bath in a tin tub."

In between filling the tub, we make love standing up while the water is heating. Leonardo Da Vinci's Mona Lisa watches us from her frame on the opposite wall with a mysterious smile, and winks.

After we bathe together in lukewarm water, Bobby Joe calls room service for dinner. He orders: Tortelloni Gustose, Scaloppine di Vitello alla Caraonte with soup and salad. I listen as he speaks, the Italian words slipping fluently from his lips, and think how much he has grown from the small town boy I knew in Marysville. Although we both changed while apart, I don't think it would be as exciting if we had grown together; gradual change, that can't be seen, never is.

He uncorks a bottle of vintage red wine and fills our glasses. We dine by candlelight in our white terry cloth robes basking in a mellow glow with jazz music playing softly in the background.

After dinner, we start playing like two children; tossing pillows at each other, pinching and chasing. He slaps my behind, throws me on the bed, runs his hand down my thigh and brings it up between my legs; we both get hotter than boiling water. I hold him tight in the right places, kiss him all over, slide my tongue slowly over his nipples, into his ears and kiss him under his arm pits where it smells strong and sweet. We make love until the break of day. Sometimes he slows down the pace and makes me beg for more until we both explode in paroxysms of ecstasy.

The next day, after a cold shower, we visit Venice. We enter the city, built on poles, aboard a water taxi. It's like a different world. Men in suits with brief cases take water taxis to work, foreigners like me are touring and in awe of the sights.

Bobby Joe and I take a gondola ride. The gondolier, a handsome Italian man dressed in black pants, and a white silk shirt with a red sash around his waist serenades us with Italian love songs as he rows. I don't understand the words, except "Amore."

We cling to each other with our arms and eyes. We're afraid to let go or look away, less we disappear into the foaming swirls arising around the gondola as it makes its' way through the shimmering water. We kiss and electrical currents move between us. As we step off the little wooden boat with its upturned front end, that reminds me of an elf's shoe, people smile, applaud and shout, "Amore." There's something about a love so palpable that brings out the best in all of us.

We have lunch at a sidewalk café overlooking the water and gondolas. Bobby warns me to guard my food from the sea gulls pecking around underneath the tables for crumbs. We can't help but laugh at the shocked look on the face of a tourist when one of the birds swoops down suddenly, and flies away with the patron's sandwich gripped firmly between its' talons.

I breathe in the fresh air. There are no vehicles to spout exhaust fumes. The sounds we hear are hushed conversations, the clinking of dishes and silverware and the barking of dogs on the square. Muted music drifts from the gondolas. Salt water enters the frothy Venetian Lagoon from the Adriatic Sea by a narrow entrance called the Porto di Lido. The smell from the sea water mixes with the spicy Italian food being served in the cafes giving off a pleasantly pungent aroma.

A jewelry store is among a row of colorful shops facing the sidewalk café. After we eat, he takes my hand and says let's browse around the shops. It's here that we select my engagement ring, a wide yellow gold band with a row of diamonds on one side of an exquisite round diamond. The gold band widens in a downward curve on the other side causing the one ring to resemble an engagement ring and wedding band blended. He slides it on my finger and whispers "Besame Mucho" in my ear. I'm the happiest woman alive.

 46

HAPPINESS AND TRUE LOVE

Every since I found Bobby Joe, I've been as giddy with happiness as a schoolgirl.

Morrie and I are flying across the Atlantic Ocean on our way home from Rome. I hold my ring finger up and let the glow from the overhead reading light set the stone glittering. I look at it, think about my last night with Bobby Joe and start giggling.

Morrie sighs. "Daughter, I've never seen you like this before. Happiness is bursting forth from you like rockets. Your joy is contagious. As soon as we get off this plane I may turn a cartwheel."

I turn and kiss him on his forehead. "And it's all because of you, Morrie. You never told me how you found him."

"Candy told me about Bobby Joe right after your first visit to The Flamingo Club. She told me the singer, Stan Crooke reminded you of him and how Bobby Joe was the only man you have ever loved and you wanted to find him. When I went home with you Christmas, I talked to Trudy Miller after dinner. She gave me phone numbers of some of his relatives. I learned which branch of the service he was in then I turned it over to a detective. Locating him was easy. But when we first found him his wife was living. None of us thought it a good idea to reunite you under the circumstances.

"My detective was notified by a contact in Rome of the death of his wife. When the detective reached Bobby Joe, he wanted to know who was searching for him. When he learned it was you, he was eager to see you. I wanted the reunion to be held in the perfect romantic setting. Because he was living in Italy, I thought the Tivoli Fountain would provide the magic moment I envisioned for you. "

"So, going to Rome wasn't your lifetime dream. You did this for me."

"Yes. You caught me. But I have never given a gift that made me so happy before."

I look at him wondering still why this little Jewish man loves me so much. I ask him again for the umpteenth time. "Morrie, I'm glad you chose me to be your daughter. The things you've done for me, the love you've shown is unbelievable. But why me?"

"Jolee, I suppose you have the right to know. I told you only half the truth. Actually, Esther and I did want a daughter. But there was another reason. I considered telling you a long time ago, but I thought it would be disrespectful to Esther's memory. I understand now to make my cleansing complete, I must respect Esther and Ericka."

"Who is Ericka?"

Morrie folds his hands, sighs and plunges in. "Jolee, do you believe it's possible to love two people at the same time? I mean for a man to love two women at the same time?"

"I don't know Morrie. I only loved one man. Bobby Joe told me he loved his wife although he still loved me and thought about me every day. So yeah, I believe it's possible."

"Ericka was a singer. She had made several recordings and was on the verge of great fame when she appeared at the Flamingo. She was a beautiful girl, shaped like a goddess, with skin as smooth and brown as coffee with a touch of cream. She sang in a throaty jazz voice that made me want to sit and watch and listen for hours. I fell in love with her even though I was married and deeply in love with Esther."

I nod, wondering which is worse, to lose your love or to have two and not be able to give up either one. The flight attendant stops and reminds us to return our tables to the upright position for landing.

Morrie continues, "We had an affair. I don't know if she loved me as much as I loved her. That's beside the point. I loved her deeply, the way you love Bobby. She became pregnant with my baby. I couldn't leave Esther and I couldn't ask Ericka to risk losing her career to have a baby outside of marriage by a Jewish man. So I arranged for her to have an abortion." He fell silent and turned his head.

"What happened to her Morrie?" I ask softly after some time has elapsed.

"The abortionist used dirty instruments. Ericka developed an infection and died."

Tears are steaming down Morrie's face. I cradle him in my arms. "I'm sorry, Morrie. I shouldn't have probed and caused you to relive something so painful."

"I think of it every day. The only time I find peace is when I'm doing nice things for you. You look very much like her. When I help you, I feel somehow that I'm repaying the debt that I owe her. When I help May Lilly and Cherub, in a way, I'm helping my unborn child."

Now I understand Morrie Rubenstein and feel closer to him than ever.

Before the plane lands in New York City, Morrie asks, "What's next for you and Bobby?"

"He and his daughter are coming later this year to meet my kids. We plan to get married next spring. We will live in Detroit."

"Great. I hear he took courses in business administration in the army. I need a son to help manage my businesses. An old man like me needs to rest."

I laugh. "Morrie, you will never be an old man. But you may need to rest after the workout that hot Italian mama gave you."

He winks. The plane comes in for a landing with us laughing and happy as two kids returning from Disneyland.

Epilogue

Time has passed swiftly like birds flying south for winter, bringing with it many changes.

Bobby Joe and I were married on April 17, 1963 in Detroit where we continue to live. Morrie employed Bobby to manage the show bars and market before he died ten years later. Morrie's estate, except for a grant to Jewish Charities, was left to us.

I obtained a bachelor's degree in nursing and went on to earn a master's in psychiatric nursing. May Lilly is a psychologist and Cherub a social worker. Bobby Joe's daughter, Angelina became a jazz musician. She splits her time between Detroit and Italy.

Morrie would be pleased to know that we used a large amount of the money he left us to develop a home for abused women and their children. Our family works to help women escape from abusive men. Some of the women are in life threatening situations. I have been there so I know it's not easy to leave without a network of resources.

The huge comfortable home is outside Detroit on a large tree lined lot. There is no name on the building and the women sign a pledge to never reveal the location. I work on healing their bodies and minds from wounds that have been inflicted by lovers and husbands — men they loved and thought loved them in many cases.

Cherub is devout in her mission as a social worker. She and her staff of six other social workers make routine visits to hospital emergency rooms and police stations, reaching out to women who have been abused. Many of them come to us with children. As a child psychologist, May Lilly evaluates and helps the children overcome the horrors and fear that have taken root in their young minds from enduring abuse and witnessing their mothers' abuse.

We have developed an underground railroad of safe houses to help women who have to leave the Detroit area for their safety. We work with the federal government to place them into the witness protection program using identity change when it is absolutely necessary for their survival.

With the changes brought about because of the Civil Rights Movement, black customers were free to go anywhere they chose. Black entertainers could make more money recording, playing concerts and Vegas. The Flamingo began to lose money and so Bobby Joe closed it. The small jazz lounge that Morrie loved is still open and Bobby's daughter appears there often.

Bobby Joe oversees the management of the safe house program and he still runs the market. We keep it for sentimental reasons. If it hadn't been for the store, I wouldn't have met Morrie. If I hadn't met Morrie, I may still have the bullet in my heart or died as a result of it being there. And Bobby Joe wouldn't be by my side.

The market is a survivor, just like me. During the 1967 riot, it was the only store on the block untouched by fire or looters. Morrie was still living then. I think it was largely because of the love and respect the community had for him that it was left unscathed.

We kept Morrie happy and comfortable when he began to fail. He never was alone or placed in a nursing home.

It was God's plan that Joel stayed in White Chalk. Like Moses in Egypt land, Joel became the savior of the people of White Chalk. John El taught him what he knew about running the business and then sent him to school to advance his knowledge in business management. When Joel grew up, John El stepped back and allowed him to implement the knowledge he gained in school and his natural compassion for people.

My son is more like me than his father.

He follows all of the government requirements for a clean environment. The air in White Chalk is clean and people no longer cough themselves to death. Joel pays fair wages and benefits including health insurance. Despite the high cost of doing business— production, sales and profits have increased tremendously. Chalk from the Murphy Mine is shipped all over the United States and Canada. Milk and butter from the dairy farm is shipped throughout the south.

Joel and his family visit us in Detroit. But he will never leave White Chalk and his dad. He still walks with a limp that must be a constant reminder of the day John El shot me in the heart and crashed a bullet into his leg. Still, he adores his father. It is beyond my comprehension but I guess he and God understand and forgave.

John El remarried after he got out of prison to a full-grown woman. She's half his age but she was twenty-five when they married, which was a step in the right direction. I hear he's not nearly as mean as he used to be. I think Joel has been a good influence on him.

As for me, I still wake up screaming at four every morning.

Bobby Joe wraps his arms around me, brushes the cold sweat gently from my forehead and speaks softly to me of love in sweet Italian words with a slight southern accent, until I drift back to sleep in the safety of his arms.

It's been over forty years since we found each other in Rome. When I wake up with him by my side and he whispers "Besame Mucho," the excitement is still new. Nothing except death will ever separate us again.

Printed in the United States
215137BV00001B/7/P